THE GOLDEN AGE SOCIETY
AND OTHER STUDIES

By the same author:

Radicalism on Campus: 1969-1971

THE GOLDEN AGE SOCIETY
AND OTHER STUDIES

by

Mona G. Jacqueney

PHILOSOPHICAL LIBRARY
NEW YORK

Copyright, 1978, by Philosophical Library, Inc.,
15 East 40 Street, New York, N.Y. 10016
All rights reserved
Library of Congress Catalog Card No.77-087939
SBN 8022-2219-6
Manufactured in the United States of America

To the Memory of Anna Gnatt

Contents

Introduction ix

1. The Golden Age Society: A Participant Observation Study of the Elderly in Long Beach 1

2. 23 Jews from Recife: Attitudes and Prejudices in New Amsterdam 71

3. A Comparison of Two Societies: Israel and the People's Republic of China 113

4. The Community College: Issues & Priorities for the 70s 145

Introduction

The Golden Age Society was written during the Spring of 1968 under the guidance of Dr. Hyman A. Enzer, Chairman of the Social Science Department of Hofstra University.

My goal was to look into the phenomenon of the changing demography of the population of Long Beach, New York and to understand the reason for the change in Long Beach from an active Summer resort for many years to where the hotels became a residential establishment catering to the needs of the elderly. I also sought reinforcement of my thesis that the life of an individual revolves around four stages: childhood, adolescence, adult life and finally, the Golden Age. The theme of the study is taken from an interview: "There is always a crying need for companionship, regardless of age. The whole life is the art of managing. Society looks to the individual who has within himself or herself the capacity to make someone happy. Why should it dry up? Love or companionship, or call it what you like, it is still the best thing in life."

The other essays included here—The 23 Jews from Recife: Attitudes and Prejudices in New Amsterdam; A Comparison of Two Societies: Israel and the People's Republic of China; and The Community College: Issues and Priorities for the 70s—evolved out of my doctoral studies in the Sociology Department of New York University, Graduate School of Arts and Sciences.

The Golden Age Society

I live in the city of Long Beach. It is a city of five miles of white sand beach situated on the South shore of Long Island fronting on the broad Atlantic Ocean. Originally a summer resort, Governor Whitman signed a bill in 1922 making it a city. The all-year-round population comprises about 30,000 with an additional population of almost 100,000 during the summer season. Considered an all-year fine climate, Long Beach is especially comfortable during the hot summer. Within a 45-minute commuting distance from New York, it is described by the Chamber of Commerce as "America's Healthiest City."

It is a predominantly middle-class Jewish community, balanced by a smaller Catholic and Protestant population, a small Negro community and an even smaller Puerto Rican group, that have filtered in over the last dozen years. There are 9 temples, Orthodox, Conservative and 1 Reform. It also includes two Catholic churches, a Baptist church, a Lutheran church, a Christian Science church and the St. James Episcopal Church. There are over 100 social and cultural groups in the community. Among them are the American Cancer Society, American Israeli Lighthouse, the Dad's

Club, B'Nai B'rith, P.T.A., etc. Long Beach has four elementary schools, Lido, East School, Central and West School, a junior and senior high school. There is a Youth Bureau, composed of a cross section of the city's population. Its members include public officials, educators, clergymen, businessmen, professional people and other citizens. There is a Charter Review Committee, a Planning Board, a Commission on Human Relations, a Recreation Commission, a Housing Authority and a Citizens Advisory Committee. Long Beach is a "democratic" town with a city manager. There is an adult education program, an Art Association and many choral groups. For the older citizens, there is the Golden Age Group, a private organization which is actively supported by the community.

Up until 1957 the 16 hotels in the town received their clientele from the middle class urbanites of New York City, Brooklyn, Bronx and New Jersey. There was the appeal to middle-class families where the father who worked in the metropolitan area during the hot summer months could rejoin his family down at the shore within an hour's travel. These hotels no longer get their clientele from these areas. A phenomenom changed this. The changing demography of the aged is the cause. Allan Nevins describes demography as "a scientific study of all kinds of human tendencies and processes, from the laws which control marriages to the facts regarding population mobility, and to the morals as revealed in illegitimacy rates."[1]

Back in 1957, the Scharf family, long active in the Brooklyn area in hotel living for the elderly, ventured into Long Beach, recognizing the growing need for providing fitting accommodations and community living to suit the individual needs of older citizens. The Scharfs were so successful with their first hotel, the Royale, which caters to up to about 200 guests, that they ventured into a second, and a third hotel, with equal success. Other hotels also began to recognize this growing need. Plainly visible too was the guaranteed financial success. With the exception of two, the hotels all followed the pattern of converting their facilities over entirely to serving the needs of the aged. The guests comprise widows, widowers and couples. In the case of couples, many have met at the hotel where they reside. Here is an example of the kind of advertising the hotels employ to reach the public: "a home away from home for mother or father in a warm, friendly atmosphere, special diets; all the comforts of home with none of the cares and responsibilities; new 100% fireproof hotel, designed to enhance the golden years, delicious homecooking, dietary laws observed, magnificent air-conditioned lobby, handsomely decorated, carpeted rooms with telephone, card room, T.V., movies, art instructions, daily entertainment." Some hotels even advertise limousine service to New York City and add the phrase "for active retirement living."

In visiting one of the larger hotels, I made it a point to check the menu list and found the dinner menu invited a choice of more than a dozen of meat and fish items from which to choose. The hotel lobbies I visited are painted in bright cheerful colors. Visible were tended green philodrendron and other house plants. Sometimes I visited in the morning around 11 A.M. Usually I found small groups sitting around. Both English and Jewish newspapers were visible. A visit to the outer porches (of the smaller-size hotels) revealed a similar pattern of behavior. Some guests were relaxing quietly, a few in groups, discussing television programs, their grandchildren (a favorite subject with the elderly) and some the cost of living. Walking into the television room at any time, whether it was before noon or in the afternoon, I joined the Golden Agers in watching some of their favorite programs. Art Linkletter's program was one of their special favorites. It was not uncommon for the person sitting next to me to share his or her feelings with me and comment about Art Linkletter and the guests on his program. They were especially pleased when younger children appeared on the program, and expressed out loud how one youngster or another resembled one of their grandchildren. It tickled them when a child said she minded her teacher more than she minded her mother because the teacher could send her to the principal for punishment. It didn't matter from what corner of the room the comment came. You got the definite feeling of audience participation from the house guests at all times.

Introduction to Hotel Owners

One clear sunny afternoon towards 2 P.M., I walked into the L hotel, approached the desk and asked to see one of the owners. When she approached me, I explained I was doing a participant observation study of the elderly and I hoped to secure her permission to visit the hotel and mingle with the guests. There was a mixed look of both interest and suspicion on her face. I had to work hard to convince her I would not mention the name of the hotel as she wished nor would I mention the names of her guests, and she finally consented.

We had hardly concluded our conversation when a well-dressed woman, white-haired with good strong facial features and of ample build, came up to me and asked me in clearly enunciated English with a Boston accent if I was a writer. In the next moment she invited me to join her in listening to her favorite afternoon show, the Art Linkletter program, and perhaps we could have a cup of tea later and chat a little more. We went into the T.V. room where all eyes fell upon me since I was a newcomer. My hostess proudly ushered me down the first row and asked me to sit in the center seat next to her. She quietly introduced me to the other two women guests who were sitting next to me. While the program was going on, she quietly whispered: "My husband was a famous physician in New York City at Mt. Sinai Hospital for more than twenty years. He was an outstanding internist. Do you know," she continued, "the hardest thing for me after losing my husband was getting used to this type of hotel. It is a first-class hotel, but the guests are predominantly Jewish. My husband and I were accustomed to living in a professional atmosphere of research people and medical people. It is so different, but what can you do? I had to get used to it, and I am contented now. You are very sympathetic. I will tell you something I could never believe of myself. I have been living down at the hotel here for the past four years. I never thought I would ever go out with any other man than my husband. Well, there was Mr. S., a guest here at the hotel. He, too, is very fond of music. Everybody calls him my boyfriend. How vulgar? He is a fine gentleman, he is about 76, polite, well-read. Do you know we have been going to the concerts at Hofstra University? I really did not think I would find this companionship here. It is good. I am not against remarriage. It is only that I never thought of it before.''

She concluded by inviting me to join her in the next room for tea. "Just look at those two gentlemen at the next table," she said, as we were enjoying our tea together, "it's the usual thing, happens every day, one of them is losing at cards, and he is accusing the other of cheating. Just when will they grow up. The one on my left is 90 and his partner is 84. That's life."

"I guess you want to know how I like living at the hotel and how I spend my time. Well, I have my newspapers and my books. My two daughters, one is a social worker, and the other is a teacher. They are both married. They visit and keep me well supplied with best sellers. My husband left me comfortable and that is a good thing not to have such worries. Twice a week, a bus picks us up and we go down to the Golden Age Club. I spend my afternoons there making ceramic trays for the hospital bazaar. There is a dancing instructor here at the hotel, and although I don't dance anymore, you should see some of the other guests. There are plenty of them taking dancing lessons. You should see them, it's a lot of fun."

She concluded our interview with the following:

"I have something special to tell you. My husband was a prominent doctor. It is so important in life to accomplish what you set out to do. I am satisfied my husband accomplished his goals. He fulfilled his purpose in life. He wanted to address an important group of research men at the medical center in Israel. We made the trip. He addressed these doctors. It was a memorable occasion. On the trip home, stopping over in Paris a few days, he began to complain about pains in his chest. His health began to fail him; he was suddenly stricken with heart failure and he died before we got home."

Apartment Houses Where the Aged Reside

Not too far from the boardwalk area I found five six-story apartment houses. Because of the comparatively low rents (three rooms are from $90 to $105.00) they attracted the retired or aged couple. This type of dwelling reflected a friendly climate. One tenant, 85 years old, enjoyed baking. Her pleasure was to invite her neighbors in once a week to enjoy her ruggaluchs and deep dish apple pie. Another, a gentleman, 82 years, maintaining an apartment with his wife of the same age, liked to reciprocate with similar kindness. For years, he knocked at her door daily, in the morning, and asked if he could bring her rolls and milk from the store. A bulletin board in the lobby of the apartment house posted the social events. Card games were popular. Most of the tenants were on social security, pensions and some even had welfare assistance. They were friendly, visited one another, and also found interest in outside activities, like the Democratic Club, ORT, temple activities and other organizational type of activities. Some of the men were Masons; the women found interest in the National Council of Jewish Women or Hadassah, or other similiar type fraternal organizations.

Interview with Officialdom

I thought a visit to the Chamber of Commerce would throw some light on the phenomenon of the influx of the elderly into the community. The secretary of the Chamber of Commerce suggested direct contact with the hotel owners and the guests themselves. I asked whether a visit with the City Clerk and permission to study the marriage statistics over the past 15 years might reveal trends. She agreed, and with that encouragement, I went over to City Hall to the office of the City Clerk. He was most cordial and willing to cooperate as best he could, and gave me permission to study the marriage records which I reviewed from 1953 up to 1967. The City Clerk cooperated still further by consenting to have me interview him. These statistics and marriage trends are indicated on pages 48, 49, 50.

Question: The marriage records show there are many senior citizens here of Russian origin. Many lived under the czar. Anti-semitism was strong. There was constant fear of government and filing of papers. Do many who come to you who want to marry show this fear of "filling out papers"?

City Clerk: When a couple wants to get married, they have to come down in person and apply for the license. All marriages in the City of Long Beach are applied for and recorded in this office. Some are senile, they cannot walk upright, they walk with canes. Others cannot speak English. In that case, we have to have a member of the family sign an affidavit.

Question: Is there the possibility that some, because they do not believe in civil marriage, may try to be married by the rabbi and avoid recording it in City Hall?

Answer: Naturally, that is no marriage, and no rabbi will officiate. On the other hand, believe me, many do get together without marriage. They live at the hotel together, not as husband and wife, but like many of the young people today on campus across the country, they "shack up." It is not uncommon.

Question: I understand Congressman Lent has conducted an investigation of violations in some of the hotels where senior citizens live.

Answer: Yes, that is so. Insulin and some other types of medication have been administered by the help at some of the hotels who have not been properly qualified to do so.

Question: What safeguards are being considered to handle these violations?

Answer: Congressman Lent and Assemblyman Arthur Kremer are trying to enact some legislation, whereby any of the hotels who take in senior citizens come under the health department so that the state can supervise all these hotels. After all, these hotels are not nursing hotels. They come under the regulation of hotels.

Question: Who supervises these hotels?

Answer: The city only—as hotels. But THAT ENFORCEMENT really is NOT ADEQUATE. This thing about hotels for senior citizens, IT IS REALLY SOMETHING NEW. It is a NEW IDEA, this senior citizen type of hotel.

Question: What is the significance as far as control is concerned?

Answer: Believe it or not, presently there are no real controls whatever. This includes the area of food, conditions, etc. It is not impossible that hotels may make promises to take care of guests as patients and there are no laws on the books to enforce these conditions.

Question: There is then, need for urgent legislation in this area?

Answer: There is indeed. There is definite need of legislation that will set rules and regulations. THIS IS A GROWING NEW FIELD.

Question: What effort is being made to make the senior citizen feel he is a part of the active community?

Answer: The senior citizen wants to be included. He wants to be accepted. He wants to vote. It gives him a feeling of social and political participation. The Democratic Party of Long Beach encourages this and brings them out, particularly during presidential elections. Voting is associated with youth. They want to be associated with youth. They want to feel they are still active in society. Can you blame them?

The City Clerk then suggested I interview the clerk who kept the marriage records.

Question: Would you care to comment on some of the older citizens who come down to see you to apply for a marriage license?

Answer: Some look years younger than their real age. On the other hand, others are bent over, some walk with a cane. Some cannot see or hear well, and in many instances they cannot write or speak English. Even others are confused with papers. When some show they are senile, then we have to have a member of the immediate family come down to sign an affidavit.

Question: What is the attitude of the older citizen as he comes down to apply for his second or third marriage license?

Answer: Amazing. Some of them are full of pep and still have a great appetite for life. For example, there was a woman of 80 who came in with a gentleman the same age to apply for a license. This was a year ago. It was a second marriage for both. It was funny, but she kind of hinted to me she was not too sure he was the right man for her. It was as if she sort of wanted my opinion. What could I do? She thought he was a little too stingy, maybe not thoughtful enough. Believe it or not, this same woman came back again this year with another gentleman! She said she should have listened when I suggested she think it over a little longer before marrying him. Well, she divorced this man after a few months of marriage, flew down to Mexico to get the divorce, and here she was back again to take another chance with a gentleman of 81 years.

Interview with Hotel B

Next morning around 10:30 A.M., I went to the B Hotel. It is a smaller type of hotel, not far from the boardwalk. The decor included plants, rockers and a thickly carpeted lobby. A group of elderly women were sitting in the lobby, watching a quiz program. They looked up as I entered and presented my card at the desk. Suddenly all attention centered on me. The lady at the desk, a friendly woman in her thirties, told me I could find the owner at their other hotel. I made my way to a medium size hotel. A pleasant quiet-voiced woman of about 55 greeted me. I explained I was doing a study of the elderly and asked whether I could see the owner to get his permission to interview some of the guests. She replied:

> "My brother is not here at the moment. I am in charge of this hotel. I can tell you that this is the second hotel for Senior Citizens we are involved in during our 8 to 10 years in the hotel field. There is a great need for this type of living among our older citizens.

Question: How do you explain your success in this business?
Answer: We are aware that we have to be especially sensitive to the needs of older people. After all, we are their substitute family.
Question: Is there any special way you handle these people, or is there any special service you render that makes your hotel different from others?
Answer: Yes, we are the only non-kosher hotel in Long Beach. We have both Jewish and non-Jewish guests. People like Mr.

L who is writing the life of Mrs. Roosevelt have their parents staying with us. Jan Peerce's mother was with us. We have as guests many prominent people and the parents of many prominent people. We attract the more American types.

Question: Do you feel that there is some reason why your guests prefer one type of cooking to another?

Answer: Well, the non-kosher type of cooking is not as heavy as the kosher. In many instances, there are those who have not been so kosher during their family lives, now suddenly when they are older they may turn to kosher foods. You know, it might have something to do with their conscience. Come back and see us tomorrow. I guess it will be all right.

I went in the direction of another hotel, entered the lobby and went up to the desk. It was shortly after lunch. The guests were congregating in the lobby. The owner had to be paged. When I explained the purpose of my study, he said, after a few minutes reflection: "Well, let me see, you can have my permission so long as you do not mention the name of my hotel nor the names of any of my guests nor say anything that would put our hotel in a bad light." I followed with a few questions:

Do you put forth any special effort in your management to please your guests?

Answer: Yes, indeed we do. We are a medium-size hotel, catering to no more than 75 guests. We emphasize the informal friendly home-like atmosphere. There is a tendency for some hotels to overemphasize the material things, television in every room, a large recreation room, a swimming pool. We, on the other hand, believe in the quality of interpersonal relations. We feel that is the most important thing. We stress individual needs, whether it is in attention or in the special diet requirements. We let our guests know at all times we are their substitute family. It is so important to create an atmosphere of warmth and acceptance. That is what makes people want to live. We are successful because making elderly people happy is our business. This is a second home for them. Our hotel is "freilach."

A Visit with the President of the Golden Age Club

The Secretary at the Chamber of Commerce suggested it might be worthwhile to interview the head of the Golden Age Club. I telephoned the president and followed with an interview:

Question: To what extent is your community involved in the Golden Age Club activities?
Answer: Yes, we have a wonderful group of women here in Long Beach. They give of their time and effort to give new purpose and direction to these wonderful older people.
Question: How often do you meet?
Answer: Twice a week.
Question: What kind of activities do you provide?
Answer: Our program includes arts and crafts, movies, socials, parties, trips to museums, lectures, concerts, art gallery visits, and visits to the planetarium.
Question: Is there any special method you use to stimulate interest in these areas?
Answer: Yes, indeed. Praise, encouragement, and more praise! To provide an incentive, handicraft objects are auctioned off, and the participants are invited to a special luncheon. You should see them, all dressed up, some of the women with hats too, not to be outdone by the younger women with their attractive hats at these luncheons!
Question: What is the membership of your Golden Age Club?

Answer: About 275 registered men and women. On the average there is an attendance of from 150 to 175.

Question: What are the ages of your Golden Agers?

Answer: They range from 50 to 93. We have one 93-year-old gentleman who has an active, alert mind of a 50-year-old.

Question: How do they get down to the Center?

Answer: A bus picks them up and brings them back.

Question: Is this a year-round activity?

Answer: This is a volunteer organization. It functions all year long with the exception of the months of July and August when our senior citizens conduct their own activities "down on the boardwalk" with their cronies.

Question: Would you like to talk about special activities?

Answer: We attended four lectures at Hofstra University. The subjects discussed were the origin of Hassidism and the life of three outstanding Jewish thinkers. For next year there are also four lectures. One of the subjects is "The Dead Sea Scrolls."

Question: Why the choice of these particular subjects?

Answer: These people are hungry for knowledge. They cannot get this over the television. Television is up to now too limited in the cultural area. Naturally, one of the best ways to find this out is through experiment. We had previous lectures, discussions by doctors, psychologists, on various subjects, including health. Whatever ailment the doctors talked about the Golden Ager tended to associate with some problems he had. I head this organization for 15 years and have reasonable experience to see their curiosity should be directed, their interest stimulated and maintained by other areas. Cultural areas seem very effective.

Question: In which sex or in what age group did you find greater interest in cultural activities as opposed to games or card playing?

Answer: Well, in the first place, we have found that age is not the important criterion. Age does not dampen curiosity. We have some over 50 who may be as inactive mentally as a 90-year-old physically. We have some who are over 90 years physically and they are as alert mentally as a 50-year-old.

Question: Is there more interest expressed by one sex rather than the other in different types of social activities?

Answer: Yes, we have found the men here who are predominantly Jewish to be more restless than the women. The men are not as interested in the cultural activities, such as lectures and museums. They prefer to be left alone, or play cards. The women still retain great curiosity. They want to go places more than the men. They want to learn, see, and hear. The men seem to be more restless, but the women seem to be doing more, are more actively interested in life.

Question: Are there any other activities planned for this year?

Answer: Last week, we saw "The World of Sholem Aleichem" at the Mineola Playhouse. Everyone was enthusiastic. They like shows; they want more of it. We also visited the Jewish Museum, saw the exhibition depicting the last stand of Masada. Would you believe it, our senior citizens were so thrilled with the visit to the Planetarium that we are looking to a return visit in the Fall.

Question: Could you tell me something about the way in which you handle your Golden Agers?

Answer: Yes, we treat them as "SOMEBODIES," something special. We call them by their surname, Mr. X or Mrs. X. If they express an opinion about something, we bend over backwards to comment on it favorably to encourage them. It is all a matter of sustaining their self-importance. That is the key. It is that important to be needed, to be useful, to have something to say that counts. We try to maintain a high morale in our effort to keep these individuals stimulated and happy. They are happy with us, feel wanted and needed.

Question: Why does Long Beach attract the senior citizens?
Answer: In some cases, they do not have a choice. They want to be independent and live by themselves and find the climate in Long Beach suitable to their needs. There is also the added feature that these hotels are geared to cater to their individual needs which may also be one answer. Naturally, you cannot ignore the fact that "this is a big money-making business." Some individuals prefer and can afford to have a separate room; others may share a room.

Question: Do many of your Golden Agers remarry?
Answer: They do. They are happy. Particularly, if they have been happy in their previous marriage, I see no reason why they cannot remarry. After all, they seek companionship, and what better way than through marriage.

Question: Which sex is more active in seeking remarriage?
Answer: As always, the woman. Today since they have a little more financial security they are also a little more aggressive about it. Anyhow, it hasn't changed too much since Shaw wrote "Man and Superman." Besides, they want companionship even if they are older, and maybe even sex.

This latter remark brought to mind a pertinent article in the May 1968 issue of Harper's written by Marion K. Sanders. The article discussed the Sex Research Project of Dr. William H. Masters and Mrs. Virginia E. Johnson conducted in St. Louis. The research was conducted in St. Louis cloaked in quasi-martial secrecy and five years later, their report "Human Sexual Response" was published. The research involved sex in the laboratory, 382 women between the ages of 18 and 78 and 312 men from 21 to 78 years old. Masters and Johnson had documented among other things that many postmenopausal women have a strong sexual drive, and that a man in his late seventies can be sexually effective.[2]

Interviews Outside Hotel B

Today was a bright, sunny day, a good day ahead I thought for some interviews with some of my new acquaintances among the Golden Age group. Outside the B Hotel, I found a bench occupied by two older men. I broke the ice by inquiring about the time. I followed that with the comment that I was involved in a study dealing with the Golden Age Group and that I was very much interested in learning about their general interests and attitudes. I inquired about the conditions at their hotel, how did they feel about social security benefits, did they feel they were getting a good deal from the government? This was my lucky day, for in a few minutes a third elderly gentleman came on the scene and sat with us. The three gentlemen who ranged in ages from 82, 85 and 86 years old had difficulty in keeping their tempers even, for they were competing very hard to get my attention and the answers were flying. I was especially fortunate, for they were so busy talking they did not seem to pay too much attention to my recording the interview, so my fingers flew as I recorded their comments:

First gentleman: Why write about us? We are elderly people. We have to get along somehow.
Second gentleman: I don't agree with him. I think that's an interesting thing to do. Maybe I won't tell you my age. Like he says, that is my business. It is a personal thing. Well, anyhow, when I came over here, about 65 years ago from Russia, a nickel was still worth 5¢. You could buy three herrings with that money. What could you get with 5¢ or even 10¢ today? Maybe, just smell the herring. Look at those

people in the new apartment house, next to the hotel. They tell us they pay $190 rent for a small apartment. That is outrageous.

First gentleman: So be logical. You think times are good today?

Second gentleman: So stop interrupting and listen for a change. Think it over. Aren't things really better. A lot better. In fact, I am going to say, a great deal better. Look, I was working night and day years ago to make a living for my family. All right, so I am 85 years old, so what. I had six children, God bless them; one son is a bachelor. He is 45 years old. Anyhow, I have 11 grandchildren and 6 great-grandchildren.

First gentleman, interrupting: Are you sure, you are not going to ask for our addresses? Anyhow, I had only one son. I was lazy. I have three grandchildren.

First gentleman: You know, you should not interrupt when I am talking. Anyhow, things are better today. Look, years ago, when my mother was sick, there was no money for hospitals, doctors, medicines. Now, look at me, I was in the hospital a few times. See how nice it was for me. I was covered, what did it cost me? Not a third, maybe 8 or 9 percent. Better times today, of course, and it would be much better, if it were not for the war.

Third gentleman (interrupting): This war is all a lot of politics, it's all among the large industrialists, those making things for war. They're all a bunch of crooks, even some in Washington.

First gentleman: I was talking, and you interrupted me. Well, if you do not prepare for the retirement years, you are out of luck. Of course, you should put something aside for later. It is not good to go to children, everyone knows that, even to the best children. I have good children.

The second and third gentleman felt it was all right to make a study or a research on the aged but the first gentleman persisted in asking whether it was the right thing to do. There was a suspicious note to his inquiry. He continued asking whether I was going to include the address of the hotel. That seemed to bother him a great deal.

Third gentleman: I think you are doing a sensible thing. Look at me, would you believe I am 86 years old. He is 85 and that one is 82. I have been coming to this hotel for over five years. Every time I want a little change, I just get up and come out here. I lost my wife about ten years ago. Oh, yes I would like to get married again. Why not. I just did not find the right one yet. Maybe I will, then I will get married. Hm, maybe I'll make a bris too. Maybe I'll have a son, who can tell (laughing). Anyhow, married people they say live longer. Statistics say so. Does it make a difference to be married again? It certainly does. One man had seven wives. He divorced all the seven. But he really wasn't so smart. Good company is good. He was a fool. Look at me, I was born in 1882. I have three rooms now. I am satisfied. I come here to the hotel, stay a few weeks, months, how I feel. Maybe I will meet somebody nice. If I do, I will get married. Why not? Who doesn't want company? Back in Brooklyn where I live, there was lately a business woman, I liked her, but she said to me, we could get married, but I could not touch her money. What kind of a woman is that?

You could not stop him, so he persisted: Everyone has his present, past and his future. I had a good life. I lived in Stanislav under Franz Josef. He was an angel to the people. Not like the Russian government. We Galitzyanner people are modest. We Jews had a chance to study. The Russian girls were crude. Their government was anti-semitic, they did not have a chance to be educated. But our women went to school.

Well, anyway, America is even better. Even a Jew could be a vice president now. I have been a democrat all my life. Look, you see that woman sitting out there on the bench there. She is 93 years old. She is tiny. See him, he is 92. They do not believe in marriage. They live together. They are happy. He knocks at her door every morning and he says: "Here I am." He brings her a glass of milk. Five years ago she was still nicer. I have been coming here for five years now, on and off. You wonder what we think about. Well, I am thinking about the war. The people do not want it. It is just that little bunch that are interested in making profits. Now about medicine, 50 years ago when you had the flu, that was the end of you. Today you got everything. People will live to over 100. Maybe over that age. I'll tell you. Some doctors tried to find out why some people live long. One doctor spoke to one man who smoked a pipe and who was 110 years old. The doctor asked him how long he was smoking. The man said, I never stopped and never will. Another doctor noticed an old man coughing. He told the doctor I have been coughing for 90 years. To the third guy the doctor asked, "Do you drink whiskey" and the man replied: "I have never stopped." The answer is you cannot really find out too much. Each person is an individual in himself. When your time comes, your lamp goes out. Everyone has a lamp. When your lamp burns out, somebody says: "Johnny, come here. It is time to go." I think it is harder for the rich than others. They live too soft. I worked hard for 72 years. Work does not harm. I could have worked until 80 but I did not want to. How do I spend my time? Well, I shop, there are groceries, meat and things to buy. There is television, and there is always a newspaper. I am not like some others. I tell you true things that can help you in writing your book. I appreciate your letting me talk to you. I am in favor of lectures and study for older people. Why not. Let me tell you, my dear, something about the nature of people. When you are born, you are either born good or bad. If you are born bad, you are born that way and you cannot help yourself. You are rotten from top to bottom. Now, my nature, and the nature of my children God bless them, they have the same nature as me. If we could help, we would even go through fire for others, but some are rotten. About 40 years ago, I was working in ladies coats, so one guy comes over to me, an older "mench" about 60 years, and he asks me, could you take me up to your place? I am an old man. I went to the boss and said I have a friend, so he is a little older, give him $30.00 and let him work. If you say so, said the boss. So I did most of the work for this man. I gave him new life. Honest to God. We did piece work. Remember that. Well, it happened I got sick and had to stay home a little. When I went back to the shop, what do you think the skunk did? If he were a few years younger, maybe four or five, I would have killed him. He went ahead and told the foreman the Italian girl who worked in our section is much faster than me, so why keep me? Nu, wouldn't you want to kill him too? Still I would help people now, even with my life. If you are born with a good character, you cannot help it, and if you are born with a bad character, you cannot help it either. Every animal has his nature. A tiger is born right away to kill. People are the same way. Some people are born good, others cannot help it, they are born bad.

Interview On the Boardwalk

One day, I was sitting on the boardwalk with my dog Pal, a "retired" husky of about 17 years, ruminating about my study when a striking tall gentleman about 6 feet 2 inches, weighing about 210 pounds sat down on the same bench. He sat right down in the middle of the bench. I was sitting on the extreme right of the bench and the extreme left was occupied by another elderly gentleman. I remarked politely to the newcomer: "I am glad you sat down, for you are doing a nice job of balancing the weight of the bench." To this remark, the gentleman replied: "Do you live here all year round? I just moved in to this apartment house on Shore Road about three months ago. Believe it or not, I am a young 78 years old. My wife who is the same age still keeps house. We occupy a beautiful three room apartment here. We like it in Long Beach, particularly so, because our apartment faces the ocean. It is a good community to live in, especially when you think of relaxed days ahead. I was born in Roumania, so was my wife. I came to this country in 1910. Why did I come here? Because America is a land of opportunity. I just retired from business. I had a very profitable printing business. I just thought it was time to take it easier. In fact, I used to live in Elmont. I built the temple there. I gave them their rabbi. Oh, you know their rabbi, too. He is indeed a wonderful man, he has great leadership and can inspire people. That is a wonderful quality, so few have it. I was active in Elmont for 15 years. I helped to build up the community culturally and spiritually. It was time to retire, to do less in business.

I asked if he had plans at this time and he replied: "It is time my wife and I found new interests. Perhaps, we will take a leisure trip to Europe first. Later, we might join one of the temples in town, or maybe some of the organizations. Anyhow, it is a wonderful feeling that we do not have to worry and that we can plan ahead for new things of interest for us to become involved in. Naturally, in the past when I was involved in civic affairs, I took on a great deal of responsibility. Now, I want more of the pleasure side of life."

Interviews at Another Hotel

Question: Good morning, are you a guest at this hotel?
Answer: Yes.
Question: How do you find living here?
Answer: How should an elderly woman find it? It is all right. I came here because I have arthritis in my ankles. You know, it takes all kinds of people to make a hotel too. Health is important. If you feel all right, everything is all right. I am 83 years. There are lots of people over 90 at this hotel. Women and men. Lots of couples who can hardly walk. Some have had three wives and are even looking for the fourth. Such old people who are getting married today.
Question: Do you approve of these marriages?
Answer: For my part, it does not matter. Good luck to them. They have everything here at the hotel. They do not have any work to do. Everything is done for them. They just come down to eat three times a day. There is somebody to make up the room. No worries, what can be bad. So they want to get married, see. Such old people too. You look at them. My God, oh well. They want to have a friend, so they get married. A lot of them walk with canes too.
Question: How do they manage?
Answer: They get social security and a lot of them get welfare assistance and they stay here. They get everything they need.
Question: Do you think this is enough to manage?
Answer: Yes it is. They get social security, and if they do not have enough, the welfare helps.
Question: Do you feel these hotels serve a good purpose?
Answer: Yes they do. Look at me, I came here suffering with arthritis in my ankles. Now I am walking. I feel fine. These hotels serve a good purpose. Here they have everything. I do not have to cook, keep house, do anything. I get three meals a day. I have no worries. It does make you look to get married.

Since I have been here, there were several marriages. My husband died when he was 57 years. That was almost 25 years ago. Now, up to lately, I had a place of my own. Now, I am living here at the hotel. It is different. Certainly, they have everything here. The men do seek lady friends, they need a friend. Some of them are crippled, yet they get married.

Question: Do you find anything unusual about this?

Answer: I really never saw anything like this, especially their wanting to get married. How long do they have to live? They want a partner. One woman just came from the hospital. It's a funny thing. She is deaf, he is blind. She just sat down at the table and told the man she liked him, and would like to marry him. It's like she just stopped the show, or she got her man or something like that. Anyhow, I think that is very funny just to sit down and in a short time to tell the man you would like to marry him. Very funny. I see you are writing down what I am saying. Some of the people at the hotel think I am a little bit of a snob because I do not talk to everyone.

Question: Are you happy with the service here?

Answer: Yes, it is a clean place. The food is good, you can get good medical attention. A lot of people eat too much and then they need help. Now, you do have to be down for breakfast at 8:00 A.M. I would not mind this too much if I had a different room partner. My partner, she is over 90 years. She likes to retire at 8:30 P.M. Who wants to go to bed so early? She also does not like fresh air. She is old. She has been at this hotel over 2 years. What I miss most is the pleasure of my television set. The management has promised me that after the Passover Holidays I will get a better room and will be able to enjoy my favorite television programs. That is a wonderful thing for everybody. The world does not pass you by when you have a television set. I will get used to staying here when I will have a better partner. What can be bad if you have a clean room, good food, no worries, the boardwalk for exercise and a beautiful view of the ocean, even sex if you want it.

Question: Have you thought of remarrying since you came here?

Answer: As I told you, I also lived with one of my daughters for 10 years during World War II and helped her because her husband who had been a soldier was killed in the war. I did not think of remarrying, but in the time I have been at the hotel, I must say it is most unusual the way it is happening here, but it is good. There are no worries, everything is good, so you think of a friend, so maybe you want to get married. It makes you feel something special.

I thanked this woman and moved off in another direction to interview another guest.

Question: May I help you with your chair?

Answer: Thank you. You are new here. Are you visiting someone, or are you here for some other reason?

Question: Frankly, I am interested in learning more about the life of the retired individual and it would be nice if you could help me.

Answer: How can *I* help you? (sigh) I am 69 years old. I have been living at the hotel for about 6 months. My husband died about 8 months ago, he was 74. He was stricken with a coronary, rushed to the hospital in the Park Slope section of Brooklyn where we lived. He never recovered.

Question: How long were you married?

Answer: We had 49 wonderful years together.

Question: What kind of work did your husband do?

Answer: During the early years of our marriage, I helped him by working in the fabric department of A & S. It gave my husband a chance to work himself up in his own textile business. It was a good business, but along came one brother-in-law, he was a scoundrel, he became a partner, and not only walked off with a lot of cash from the business, but he also took with him the wife of one of the other partners. That there are people like this scoundrel in the world who can get away with such things is unbelievable. And I am not making any of this up. It is like something you read in story books. Anyhow, if you listen to some of the life stories of some of us, I think they are better than what you sometimes find in a book. What troubles! Anyhow, we had such a good life together. He waited on me hand and foot. Nothing was too good for me. It is hard sometimes to face life when you have had so much devotion.

Question: How do you find things at this hotel?

Answer: Well, you know how it is. There will always be some people you can never satisfy. And there are always a few who will not get along with others. When I came here, I told my daughter I will try my best to make the best of it and be satisfied.

Question: What do you do to keep busy?

Answer: Well, the boardwalk is a life saver. I like to walk, and sometimes I ask one of the other guests to join me. After a while, you learn which of the ladies or gentlemen are friendly and with whom you can talk. There is a television in the lounge and you can always find a card game if you want. I am still looking for a good poker game. Does it sound funny at my age? I think poker is still a lot of fun. You forget yourself and you can have a good time, and it doesn't cost too much. You can spend the whole morning or afternoon and only lose a dollar or two. Isn't it worth it?

Question: What is your attitude towards remarrying?

Answer: The way I still feel now with my husband gone so recently, I don't know. I can just say at this hotel in the last two months we had a few weddings. One bride was in the 80's and so was the groom. You see that well-dressed gentleman walking along the boardwalk. He is the groom. He is nicely dressed, isn't he. Believe me, he's strong and healthy. We have a temple in the hotel and a rabbi. All the guests at the hotel were invited to the wedding. You should have seen the "chussin," that's Jewish for groom. You should have seen how he broke the glass, did he "hock" it to pieces! There's still plenty of life in him. Good for him. I give him credit. Do you know what one of the male guests said to me at the reception? If you will live at this hotel long enough, you will find you will have a long happy life. Well, I'll see. I cannot see it today. He says life begins whenever you are ready for it. Do you know, one of the new brides is actually doing her own cooking? She is really in her 80's, believe it or not.

Question: Do you approve of remarrying?

Answer: Why not, if you find what you want. Most of the time it is companionship. It is good to feel somebody special is interested in you. Other times you have to be careful. She could still be a golddigger even at 80 and what's the matter with some men, they still like the idea of marrying a rich widow.

*   *   *

One afternoon, I met an elderly woman coming along from the direction of the shopping area. She was pulling a shopping cart which was much too heavy for her and it was spilling over with packages. She could hardly lift it onto the sidewalk. Approaching her, I asked if I could be of assistance. "No, thank you," she replied. "I can manage despite my 72 years. My husband usually accompanies me. But today, he does not feel so well. Actually, I got all this shopping done because I wanted to be free tomorrow to keep my steady appointment at the hairdresser. You know it's important for a woman to look her best."

I asked permission to accompany her, saying I was going in the same direction, and began my questionnaire:

Question: Do you live nearby?
Answer: Yes, I live in the big apartment house over there.
Question: We are neighbors. Do you know a Mrs. X? She lives in your apartment house. I know her well. She is in her late 70's, a kind woman, who is very devoted to her husband. I believe he is her second husband. They recently returned from their Florida vacation. He has not been feeling well lately.
Answer: Oh, yes, I do believe I know her slightly.
Question: You said your husband usually accompanies you. I do hope he is not very sick.
Answer: Actually, he has a slight cold. I thought it best for him to rest indoors. Confidentially, he is my second husband. Would you care to hear how we met?
Interviewer: I am very much interested.
Answer: Well, four years ago I was living on X Street. You see, I lost my husband about six years ago. I had a nice three room apartment. Do you know that particular apartment house caters to retired couples, widows and widowers? The rent is moderate. I was paying $95.00 for three large rooms. We had a recreation hall where we could play cards any evening and meet other members of the house. They have parties, socials, Christmas and New Year affairs. Anyhow, there was this neighbor, he was a widower. We were the same age. We often met going to the incinerator. I knew there were many of the neighbors interested in marrying him. It may sound funny, but the way it comes out it was romance at the incinerator, but there's where it started. We seemed to like one another, and he proposed to me. I'm glad we had an incinerator. Do you know the kind of work I used to do? I used to be an operator on dresses before I got married. At the time I met my second husband, we were both paying $95.00 a month rent. When we decided to get married, we figured out it was smarter to move to a better house and have a little more comfort.

Question: How do you manage?
Answer: Look, we both have social security. I worked a little while before too. My husband has a little income from some investments.
Question: May I ask how you feel about your second marriage?
Answer: I am very happy. Why shouldn't I be? My husband is very attentive. Believe it or not, sometimes it is not good to be too good to your wife.
Question: What do you mean by "too good?"
Answer: My husband is overly concerned about me. Wherever I go, whatever I do, he is so concerned. When my first husband passed away, it was getting used to one way of living. Now that I found a new partner who is the concerned type, it is another thing to have to get used to his ways. But that really is not so bad. We are happy together.
Question: Judging from your personal experience, would you recommend a second marriage?
Answer: You can see from what I say that it is very possible even at our age to marry again and make a new life. I better hurry on. You know, my husband will wonder where I have been all this while even if I do come home with all this shopping.

* *
*

Leaving her, I went on to the boardwalk. Where could I find a different point of view or something new to understand about the aged? Just a short distance from the C hotel, I took the liberty of approaching a well-dressed elderly gentleman who sported a well-trimmed grey goatee. Somehow, I felt he did not speak English. Mustering the very best Yiddish I could employ for the occasion, I apologized for intruding and explained I was doing a study of the life style of the elderly in Long Beach and wondered if he would care to help me. Speaking only in Yiddish, he said this was an interesting thing to do and that he would be glad to assist me.

Question: Do you live here all year round?
Answer: Yes, I live at the D House. I have been living there about nine months.
Question: You impress me as being a gentleman of higher education. Would you care to tell me what your profession is, or are you retired?
Answer: Actually, I am retired at present. I am a Talmudist. I used to be a "shoicherd." You must know what a "shoicherd" is. I was educated and trained in Russia in this profession of following the religious rules for killing chickens.
Question: Would you like to talk about how you find living at the hotel?
Answer: The food and service is good. The trouble is people eat too much, much more than they really need. Especially older people eat more than they need. Naturally, this hotel will never take the place of my former home. You have to get used to this kind of living, and sometimes it takes a while. As a widower, it's the best way for me. It gives me time to think about things. I feel we are living in troubled times. Jew and Gentile alike are worshipping false gods. They tie it to material things. That is not good. There is too much of it today. There is one other thing. Things are too good for people in America. It makes them weak. These times need a man like Solomon.
Question: To what do you attribute your good health?
Answer: People live longer today because medicine helps. The pills help. I think people could be happier, but they really don't know how. That is an art.
Question: Can you put your finger on what is wrong?
Answer: Again I say, people have too much. It is not good. Things are too easy for them. They need to eat less, have less, want more. They are too smug, too satisfied. They could learn a lot from studying the habits of the tiny ants and their society.

There is unity in their lives, organization, cooperation and harmony in that society. Yes, we could learn a lot from them.

Question: Lots of older people are marrying for the second time. How do you feel about remarrying?

Answer: It sounds sensible. There is always a crying need for companionship. It is good to feel someone special is interested in you. Someone needs you. It is healthy. Some people need this very much. Others close their feelings to it. Maybe I am one of these latter people. Right now, I am like them. I had a wonderful married life. Now I am content with my books and reflecting about life in general. Perhaps time may change my mind. I have to give myself a chance.

I thanked the gentleman and thought I might pay a visit to one of the other nearby hotels. It was teatime, around 3:30 P.M. I entered the lobby, greeted one of the owners at the desk and went into the recreation room where I secured a cup of tea at the "bar" set up for this purpose. I then went and sat down at a table. There were four other occupants at the table. I sat between an elderly gentleman on my left and an elderly woman on my right. I began the conversation by talking about the weather and soon the questions followed:

Question: How long have you been a guest at this hotel, sir? Are you comfortable here?

Answer: Have we a choice sometimes? It is all right. My children looked around quite a bit before they found this hotel. They wanted to be sure to find a place where I could feel at home. Look, what could be bad? It is not like my wife's cooking, but it is all right. There is shelter, someone to talk to. If I don't feel well, I can get a doctor right away. A newspaper is handy. If my rheumatism is not too bad, I invite a "bucher"—companion—and we take a walk. We can argue our heads off about the election. So what can be so bad.

Question: What was your profession?

Answer: I am an old-timer now. Two weeks ago, I celebrated my 78th birthday. My daughter-in-law gave me this pipe and my son surprised me with a brand new RCA television. What more can I ask out of life? I have good children. My daughter lives in Baltimore. She sent me a telegram of congratulations. You asked about my profession. I had a very successful dentist practice in Brownsville for many years. Look at what has happened to Brownsville now. It is run down, a slum.

Question: How long did you say you reside at the hotel?

Answer: It is going on three years now. You know, after a while, with no wife around to remind you, you forget about time.

Question: Speaking about your wife, have you ever thought about remarrying?

Answer: Even up to a year ago, I wouldn't have thought about it. My wife and I were very devoted. We have two children, my son is a successful buyer, my daughter is a schoolteacher. There are four grandchildren. Oh, yes about marrying again. Today we live in modern times. Every day has to count. There are some people here who have married again. I'll tell you a secret. It wouldn't be wrong to say we need as much affection or attention now as we did before.

It was time to pay attention to the woman on my right so I cast a glance in her direction and remarked that a cup of tea is so satisfying. I added: "You give the impression you have been engaged in activities other than homemaking."

Answer: Yes, indeed, I worked in a bank for more than 10 years. I did this when the children were a little older, when they went on to college. My husband really did not like me to work. I got myself this job in the bank near my home in Flatbush.

With the boys away, I had more time on my hands than I needed. I thought the best thing to do was to work, and since I like working with figures, I went down to see the vice-president at the bank and he gave me a job.

Question: How do you enjoy living at this hotel?

Answer: I have been very comfortable here. I lived at another hotel for a while. The food was a little better there. But here, the rooms are bigger. Besides, I have made so many friends.

Question: You dress very attractively and in good taste. Does this mean a great deal to you, how you look?

Answer: I believe a woman should take good care of herself. Do I look my years? I am 68. A woman pleases herself first and her husband will always find her desirable. That's a good marriage.

Question: Talking about marriage, have you ever considered remarrying?

Answer: Why not. I was married for 38 years to a good man. He was in textiles. We had a good life together. We had two children. There are 9 grandchildren. I would marry again. There is nothing wrong with looking for companionship. A woman is like a package of cereal. Each one is made up of attractive parts, and there is always a buyer for an attractive package.

A day or two later, I had a little good fortune which led to another interview. While walking up the ramp to the boardwalk proper, an older woman dropped her handbag. I hastened over, picked it up, returned it to her, and asked if I might have the pleasure of walking with her since I was going in her direction. Soon we were involved in conversation.

Question: Do you live nearby?

Answer: Oh yes, I live in an apartment on X street. Most of the occupants are either couples like us or widows in search of a husband. You should see how they are looking. It's a regular rat race.

Question: You look as if you take good care of yourself.

Answer: I'll tell you a secret. I am really 76 years old, but I tell my husband I am 72. He is 74, so why should I tell him my real age. Especially when he says I don't look a day over 65. See, that's what makes a good marriage.

Question: What kind of work did your husband do?

Answer: My husband was in wholesale fruit business. During World War II when my son went into the navy, I thought the best thing to do was to go out to work, so I went to work in a dress factory as an operator. Rather than the doctor tell me to go to work to keep my mind busy, I knew what to do. You know, my husband was against it, but a woman sometimes has to go against her husband's wishes, especially if she knows what is best for her health.

Question: How do you and your husband manage?

Answer: Well, I get around $80.00 a month and my husband about $120 from social security. This and Medicare is enough for us to get along.

Question: How much rent do you pay?

Answer: We have three nice rooms. We pay $105.00 a month. Our three children wanted to contribute towards this but my husband and I are independent. We would not accept any financial help. We are proud.

Question: How long are you living in Long Beach?

Answer: This is our third year in Long Beach. Before that, we lived in the Bronx. The neighborhood there is going down, so our children began to look around, and since one of our daughters lives in Oceanside, she thought we might like to live down here by the seashore.

Question: How do you manage with the shopping?

Answer: I'll tell you, my husband is retired, so we divide the chores between us. My husband is the better shopper, he looks for all the specials at Waldbaums. I do most of the house chores. My husband brings the laundry to the laundromat. We share our work and find it works out well. I guess I am telling you more than I have ever told any one about my life. Anyhow, we are happy together. We do not have too much, but we have each other. The important thing, we are grateful for what we have and we make the best of everything. You know we even find time to enjoy a snack around ten o'clock in the evening when we go back into the kitchen for a fresh bagel and cream cheese and a cup of coffee. What more can you ask for when you can have this pleasure? It is really how we make our lives that counts. We do not have too much but we make a great deal of it.

Question: Do you prefer living in an apartment?

Answer: Yes, my husband and I feel, just so long as we can manage physically, we like this style of living. My youngest daughter who bought a house in Oceanside asked us to live with her in a separate apartment on the lower floor, but my husband and I felt it was not the right thing to do. It is better for the children and the parents not to share the same house. They can work out their problems better. I am a sensitive woman. If they had problems, I would be very distressed. It is better this way.

Question: Do your children come and visit often?

Answer: Yes, and no. One daughter lives in Connecticut, so we visit and they come to see us a few times a year, especially during holidays. Our son and our other daughter live nearby and we see them about once a week when everyone is well. Last week was an especially joyous occasion. It was Passover and the children came over with the grandchildren and we enjoyed the traditional Seder. Tradition is good. The children grow on it. It gives meaning and interest to their lives. We prepare special dishes, like gefilte fish, chicken soup with knedels, roast chicken, and of course, plenty of matzoh. Our youngest grandchild who just made his Bar Mitzvah asked the four questions of the Passover Feast. We live for holidays.

Question: How do you feel about the hotels that cater exclusively to senior citizens?

Answer: They are good. They fill a need. Some people prefer the comforts and conveniences of a hotel. They do not want to be bothered with the responsibility of keeping house. Some are not so well, so it is good for them to live at the hotel. They can get medical attention, help from an attendant. Social security helps, and if you need further help, even though I do not like welfare, you can get help if you need it. One good thing, our government helps. Actually, what is the whole life, if not the art of managing?

Question: What do you think of the life here in Long Beach?

Answer: We enjoy living here. I like the ocean view. I like to walk on the boardwalk. My husband likes to rest a little more. Some people are lonely, but I am not. The time passes quickly when you are busy. I am glad to be busy and run my home.

Question: How do you feel about older people marrying again?

Answer: Like I said, the whole life is the art of managing. A woman has within her a capacity to make someone happy. Why should it dry up? Love or companionship or call it what you like, it is still the best thing in life. What more of an answer can I give you?

* *

*

The next day for contrast I visited one of the larger hotels around 11 A.M. Some of the guests were on their way out for a walk. I looked in on the television room. There were the audible comments from the houseguests about the "Personality" quiz program. Out on the sundeck were more than two dozen people, comfortably seated, enjoying the morning sun. There was quiet conversation going on. I overheard one woman say, "That was no way for a woman to behave at a hotel and the least she could have done was to realize she was among people and to have consideration for other people's feelings." Another gentleman was involved in conversation loud enough to be heard and he felt it was time to change the president.

It looked like a good time and place to strike up conversation. At first, I could see from the glances I was regarded with suspicion. I was a stranger. Finding an empty chair, I sat down and greeted the woman next to me. It was sunny. That was a good beginning. I talked about the weather.

Question: You look comfortable, how long have you been enjoying yourself here?
Answer: I live here about two years. My first room wasn't so comfortable, but the management is nice, after a while they changed my room and I am satisfied.
Question: You appear to be in good health. Do you find you get the right attention when you are not feeling well?
Answer: There is always a doctor handy when you need one. I have a special diet which they follow strictly. I am slightly diabetic. I take orinase. My waitress always reminds me not to forget my pills. Bessie is thoughtful. I am satisfied here.
Question: How do you feel about this type of living?
Answer: Like everything else, you have to get used to it. Naturally, your own home is better. But then, you get old, the children go their way. You need a place where you can have your comfort and attention and not have to worry about a roof over your head. So I am here.
Question: How do you manage?
Answer: Well, I'll tell you. I was married twice. My first husband left me a little money. My second husband died about a year ago. There is a little income from investments, pension and social security. Both my husbands were business men. I manage.

Question: Since you were married twice, would you think of marrying again?

Answer: People are not so shy as they used to be about it. My first husband used to say to me: in business, if you have something to sell, there is always someone to buy. Marriage is something like that. What is important, you have to meet the right one.

The woman seated on her right seemed interested in our conversation, and I encouraged her.

Question: How do you like it here?

Answer: To tell the truth, I was lonely at first. It is a big hotel. It took a while to make friends. Now it is better. I am here one year.

Question: What kind of work did your husband do?

Answer: My husband had his own business. He had a scrap metal business. He was a good provider. We had a home in Westchester. We married off our children well. They are all professionals. The oldest is a doctor, my daughter is a psychologist, she liked to study, and my baby is a married man now with three children. He is a pharmacist. I didn't need a home any more. When my husband passed away two years ago, the children brought me here. After all, I am 72 years. Could I take care of my home now? It is the best thing for me. I take a walk once in a while. There is always someone around to talk to. I can always find a newspaper and I like a little television in the afternoon.

Question: Would you care to tell me your opinion about second marriages?

Answer: Well, I'll tell you. It's a new thing. Who ever thought about it? I was satisfied with my marriage. My husband gave me everything. But it's funny. Since I have been living at a hotel, I see quite a few people who marry again, some even for the third time. It's something to think about.

* * *

The following afternoon, towards 2:30 in the afternoon, I was back on the boardwalk. The weather was clear, a little windy perhaps as I made my way hopefully in the direction of the P hotel. There were about a dozen occupants seated outside the hotel and I just sat down among them. Some of the women I had interviewed on other days greeted me and I acknowledged their greeting in kind. Soon I was introduced as that friendly young lady who likes to talk to people, and so here was a good opportunity for me to interview. The woman next to me was friendly and I inquired:

Question: How long are you a guest here?
Answer: About 5 months.
Question: Why did you choose this hotel?
Answer: My husband passed away eight months ago, he was 80 years. I am 78. I was so upset. My wonderful children thought it was the best thing for me to make a complete change, and I like a smaller type of hotel. I don't feel so alone.
Question: What was your previous way of living?
Answer: Up to the time my husband died, I kept house. We had a four room apartment in the Flatbush section of Brooklyn, not too far from my eldest son. My husband and I enjoyed our life together, and even after the children married, we still had each other.
Question: What kind of work did your husband do?
Answer: My husband was a waiter. He did not play cards like some of the others in the trade. He made a good living, we saved our money, devoted our time to our family and we were content.
Question: Did you work at all during your married life?

Answer: No, there was enough to do raising the family. My husband was a man of good habits, a steady worker and a good provider. My job was to raise the children. Children need a lot of your time. Years ago we did not have the gadgets you have today to save time. Something is wrong today, though. This generation wants too much. Everybody is working. Where are all the mothers? Too many of them are out working when more of them should be at home with their children.

Question: How do you find the accommodations and service here?

Answer: I have a nice, private room and the food is good.

Question: Do you find the guests to be friendly?

Answer: Well, it's like it was in Brooklyn with my former neighbors. They were friendly too. You know, you don't interfere with their privacy. You greet them good morning, and talk cheerfully about things and you can't make enemies that way. I guess people are all alike that way. The best thing is to keep your troubles and sadness to yourself. Maybe I have said a little too much to you. You have been so friendly and kind.

Question: Would you recommend this way of life?

Answer: Yes, I think it is the best for us at this stage. I have two daughters-in-law and one daughter also. When they go to the P.T.A. meetings or want to play mah jong, do you expect them to take me along? Either way, you are lonely. But this is still the best. It is healthier. At least here I find people like myself maybe we are not too happy. After all, I lost my husband not too long ago. You really feel lost. Now it is all right. I have friends.

A third woman was anxious to make some remarks so I turned to her and remarked: "The weather is a little better today than yesterday, isn't it?

Answer: We are having a Spring for a change. Everyone seems to feel better.

Question: How long are you here?
Answer: Several years, let me see, about 3½ years. When my husband died, six years ago, I lived with a daughter for a while, but I thought it would be better to find a hotel where my daughter could have her privacy with her little family and I could have mine, and I could come and go as I pleased. Life seems to show it is better that way for all of us. Besides it is more fun to visit the grandchildren. I have four, two girls, two boys. Sometimes they get me dizzy. They climb all over me like kittens. They are wonderful.

Question: Do you find companionship here?
Answer: You know it was difficult at first getting used to this new way. Over the years I made new friends. You learn to be choosy, you can find people to your taste. There is always something you have to overlook if you want to be content.

Question: How do you keep busy?
Answer: The Golden Age Club is very active in this town. The bus brings us to the center and takes us back. We have bingo, cards, arts and crafts. Sometimes we go to a lecture, sometimes we go to a museum. We went to the Jewish Museum. It was interesting. The men don't seem to like it too much. They'd rather play cards. We also go to shows. It's a lot of fun. Anyhow, they are fine people who help. They try to make us happy. They respect us.

Question: Do the men from this hotel visit the Golden Age Club?
Answer: As I told you, they look forward to their pinochle games. They forget about everybody when they find their "chavirim" and get into the card games.

Question: Would you say the men are attentive at this hotel?
Answer: Oh, yes, all the time except when they find a card game. I was invited to go walking several times with different gentlemen. We went on the boardwalk, we had tea together. It is friendly here. The management tries to make us comfortable.

Question: Do you find people here marrying again?

Answer: A short while ago, we had a nice wedding here. It was a second marriage for both.
Question: Would you think of marrying again?
Answer: So far, nobody proposed to me. I think so, it's certainly better than being alone. After all, there is a little social security, you get some help, you share a nice room. You have someone specially interested in you. What's bad?

*   *
*

One day I had a stroke of good luck. I learned about some recent marriages and thought it would be a good idea to go down and interview them at their hotel. The management of the hotel eyed me with a little concern when I explained I was doing a study of the living patterns among older people and that I would like to interview their guests. I had to reassure them that I would be discreet about what I would talk about, that I would not mention either the name of the hotel, or the names of the guests, or offend the reputation of the hotel.

I made my way out onto the porch and sat down on a rocker. Soon an elderly man and woman came by and sat down nearby. I changed my seat closer to them, and began my inquiry:

"How do you like the Spring weather we are having?"

Answer: It is a nice day, but my husband feels since I was not feeling so well the last few days I should not take a walk with him, but should sit and rest more.
Question: How long have you two been married?
Answer: About three months. It is a second marriage for both of us. We met at this hotel.
Question: Would you care to tell me your age?
Answer (husband): My wife is still young, she is just 70, but I am a little older, I am 74. We are very happy together.

Question: How do you find this type of living?
Answer (the wife): Could anything be bad about it? If you have a special diet or need special attention, you get it. My husband was not so careful about how he was eating, and he had to go to the hospital for a week. Thank God, there was nothing wrong, just older people mustn't eat too much and sometimes they have to be a little more careful of what they eat.
Question: Would you care to make a comment about remarriage?
Answer (husband): I'll tell you. Before we got married, we used to fight like cats and dogs. She was always making me jealous. I feel much better now that we are married. My wife is also much quieter too.
Question: Would your wife like to make a comment too?
Answer: What more can I say? It makes you feel like living. We are just beginning to live.

The Social Structure

The social structure of the elderly in Long Beach is seen, (1) in their different life styles,(2) socialization at the Golden Age Club and (3) their daily interaction. What does it reveal?

1. The importance of self-esteem.
2. The need for acceptance.
3. They want to be shown respect.
4. They want to be needed.
5. How important it is to be useful!
6. They still have something important to say.
7. They want to be heard.
8. Independence is important.
9. They do not want to be looked down upon.
10. They want to be included in the mainstream of society.
11. Socialization and social interaction is critical to mental health.

12. Many thrive on remarriage for a second or third time.
13. The need for companionship is strong.
14. Sex is still a strong incentive.
15. They are still eager to learn.

William H. Whyte in his study, *Street Corner Society*, saw the structure of the gang in action in the bowling alley, in the relation of the members of the gang to each other.[3] Here among the elderly it is revealed in their different lifestyles. We also see it in action at the Golden Age Club and in daily social interaction. They represent both a subculture and a group functioning as individuals. If someone is basket-weaving, she wants praise for her basket-weaving. Don't you think these baskets are beautiful? Don't you think she makes the best baskets? There is the retired editor of the New York Times, he is 87 years old. He keeps busy shredding foam rubber all day long, as his work of art. That means so much to him. But if he did the shredding all by himself, and had nobody to communicate with, it would no longer be an art form. The fact that he is getting compliments and more compliments means he is getting done what he wants and needs. The occupational therapy through the incentive of approval and praise provides the emotional climate of self-esteem.

These older people I have seen and talked with want to be counted still as individuals. In some cases they want to conform socially. Some remarry, some live together without benefit of the marriage ceremony. They want to be accepted and to be very much a part of the contemporary scene. Look at this former editor, he still has an ego and needs very much to get approval for his shredding. Now this woman who makes the baskets, her sister said she did not think her baskets were nice, but that didn't matter so much, it was the therapist who said she made nice baskets. That's what counts. The hotel managements spell it out when they advertise attention to the individual needs of their guests. The City Clerk came close to it when he said we do everything to get the older citizens out to vote. They want to vote, it identifies them with youth. "Some remarry, others just 'shack up' like the youngsters."

The elderly gentleman expressed it when he said: "Look at that woman, she is 93 years old, see him, he is 92. They do not believe in marriage. They live together. They are happy. He brings her a glass of milk." There is the attitude of the 80-year-old woman who flew down to Mexico to secure a divorce from her second husband only to return to the license bureau to marry a third time. One 80-year-old woman summed it up when she said today's senior citizens can be independent and live in their own subculture. They want to be independent but they still need the self-esteem and respect of the mainstream of society. They want to feel needed; they want to feel useful; they still have something important to say and want to be heard. They are eager to learn and want the stimulation that culture offers. There is social security, pension funds. They do not have to keep house. They can have their freedom. They can come and go as they wish at the hotels. "The men do seek lady friends, they need a friend. What can be bad if you have a clean room, good food, no worries, the boardwalk for exercise and companionship, a beautiful view of the ocean, and even sex if you want it. Everything is good, so you think of a friend, so maybe you want to get married. It makes you feel something special."

Legislation

Need for State Licensing and Inspection of Hotels for Senior Citizens in Long Beach

Interviews with Assemblyman Arthur J. Kremer and Congressman Norman F. Lent

In an interview with Assemblyman Arthur J. Kremer at his Long Beach office, I learned that conditions in the hotels had been such that there was a critical need for legislation for licensing and inspection of the hotels for senior citizens. According to Assemblyman Kremer some of the hotels had kept guests who belonged in Nursing Homes. "Guests received medical care on the premises from persons who were either unfit or not qualified who gave pills, and 'shots.' " As early as in 1966, Assemblyman Kremer said he had introduced a bill providing for the licensing and inspection of such hotels.

In conversation with Congressman Norman F. Lent of Lynbrook at his Lynbrook office, I learned that a physical survey (of some of the unlicensed senior citizen hotels prior to legislation enacted) on September 27, 1967 by Senator Lent had revealed that some of these hotels which served exclusively as residential centers were found in many cases to be unsatisfactory. It was through the combined efforts of both Congressman Lent and Assemblyman Kremer that adequate legislation was finally enacted in 1968 which brought Senior Citizen Hotels and boarding homes under the single umbrella of State control for the first time. The legislation provided that "after April, 1969 no Senior Citizen facility could operate without State licensing and inspection."

In announcing the legislation, the Committee Chairman of the Joint Legislative Committee on the problems of Public Health headed by Congressman Norman F. Lent said "From our Committee studies we have learned that we can begin breaking down the log jam in Nursing Homes and hospitals by encouraging the operation of less specialized facilities. Properly licensed and supervised Senior Citizen Hotels and other domiciliaries can fill a real need during the present shortage. They can serve as residences for older persons who are not medically disabled but who suffer the temporary or chronic disabilities of age and need some measure of assistance and medical supervision."

Summer Program for the Aged

As a Participant Observer, I was a guest at the Malibu Beach Club in Lido Beach under a special Recreation Program for Senior Citizens. Initiated during the Summer of 1968, it included busing to and from the Beach Club (not only for residents of Long Beach, but also from other towns in Nassau County). Refreshments and sandwiches could be secured at special prices.

The program included arts and crafts. There was a piano and a pianist provided by the program; the guests were encouraged to sing their favorite tunes. There was dancing too; the fox trot, the waltz and the polka were very popular dances. One elderly gentleman confessed to me after we had been dancing that he was a former professor at New York University, and that even though he was 88, he still was interested in the opposite sex. "Women still interest me," he said. Another guest, a woman, seated in a wheel chair asked me to join her in the singing. The employees, part of this special Recreation Program, appeared very much "concerned" with their role in helping to make the Senior Citizens happy. Dr. Carol Lucas Commissioner of Services for the Aging, headed this special recreation program. She has been ministering to the Town of Hempstead's senior citizens clubs and helping older residents with problems ranging from noisy neighbors to finding a judge to perform a free marriage ceremony for a pair of golden agers with limited funds. Dr. Lucas said she was basically drawn to this program and involved in this type of activity because "nobody wanted them."

Housing for the Aging in Long Beach

Mr. James L. Bifulco, Executive Director of the Long Beach Housing Authority, informed me that the Long Beach Housing

Authority was undertaking a program which included 170 units for the elderly. Of these 105 units would be the efficiency type while 65 would be one-bedroom. Plans included a clinic, parking space, a paved, sitting area, shuffleboard courts, bocci courts, horse-shoe pits and planting areas.

Marriage Statistics in Long Beach 1953 to 1967 Inclusive

Age	Sex	Total Marriages
50-59	F	105
50-59	M	108
60-69	F	93
60-69	M	122
70-79	F	13
70-79	M	49
80-84	F	1
80-84	M	7
85-90	F	0
85-90	M	1

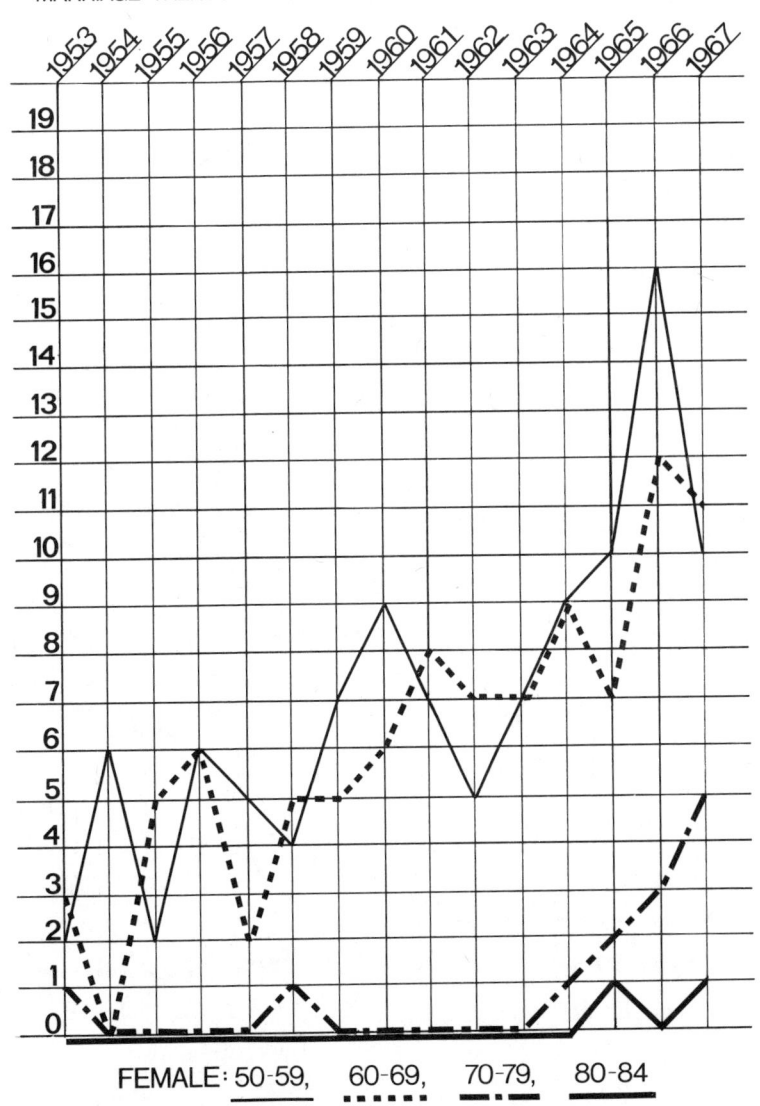

MARRIAGE TRENDS IN LONG BEACH FROM 1953 TO 1967 INCLUSIVE

FEMALE: 50-59, 60-69, 70-79, 80-84

MARRIAGE TRENDS IN LONG BEACH FROM 1953 TO 1967 INCLUSIVE

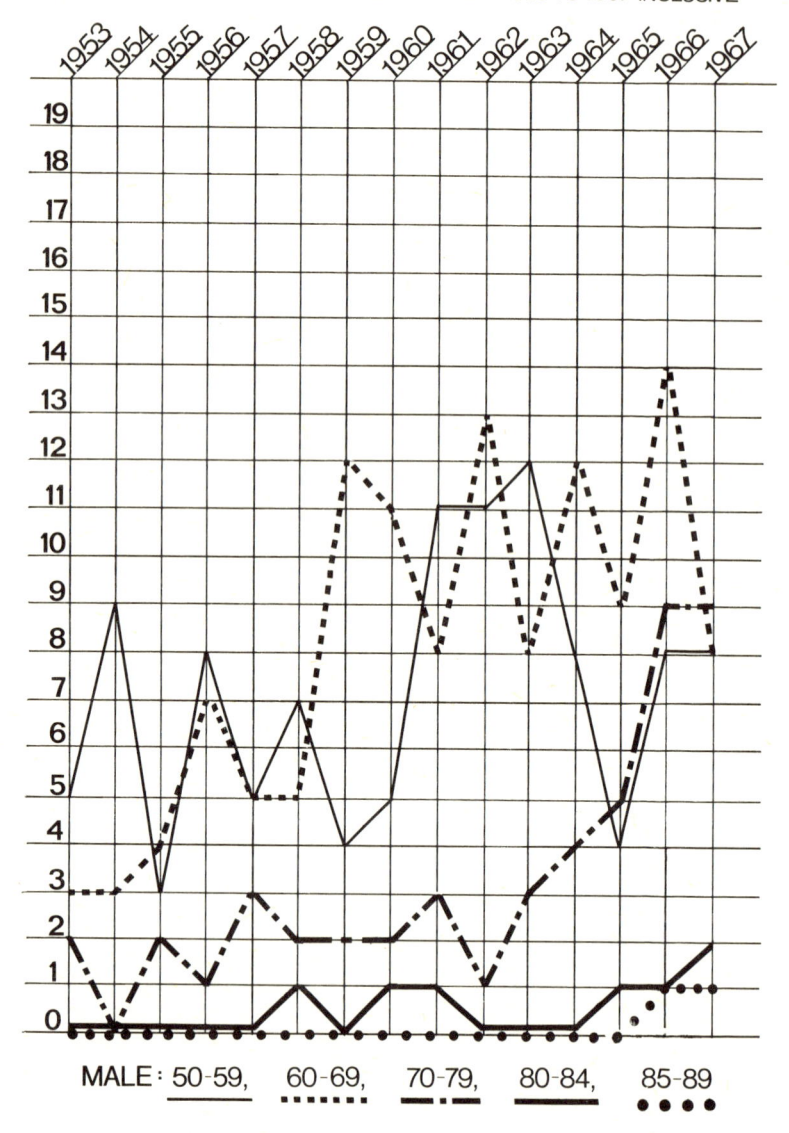

MALE: 50-59 ———, 60-69 ·······, 70-79 —·—·—, 80-84 ———, 85-89 ••••

Part II

Government Facts ... New Attitudes ... Future Trends Concerning the Elderly

The Federal Government set aside the month of May to honor its senior citizens and designated May as Senior Citizen Month. There are over 1,000 senior citizens who are 100 years, according to an announcement over nationwide television.

In 1958 the Federal government felt the need to develop a blueprint for an action program to meet the needs of the older population. On January 8, 1958 Representative John E. Fogarty of Rhode Island introduced a bill which became the White House Conference Aging Act. This conference was to serve to emphasize the problems of aging and their importance, and also serve to stimulate the interest and participation of people throughout the country. The Act invited each state to collect facts about its older population, inventory its present resources and facilities, locate and identify through analysis of the facts where services to the elderly were adequate and where there were gaps. Each state was also asked to develop recommendations for new approaches and programs to provide a basis for discussion and consideration at the White House Conference. Federal grants were made available to the states to assist them in organizing their activities as part of the Federal policy to work jointly with the states and their citizens toward a common goal.

Studies revealed that the number of older people in this country has increased five times since 1900. The middle-aged sector of the population has increased three and a half times. This growth rate far outranged the general population expansion and dramatically changed the age distribution in our society. Older people were 4 per cent of the population in 1900 and 9 per cent of it today. Middle-aged people were 14 percent of the total in 1900 and are 20 percent of it today. Collectively, the proportion of 18 percent in 1900 has become 34 percent in 1960.[4]

Over the first half of this century, the life expectancy for both men and women at birth increased greatly. For women, this expectancy has increased 20 years. Among the elderly, the women consistently outnumber the men, and the trend of the differential rate is increasing. It is now estimated that at 75, 7 out of 10 women are widowed compared with 4 out of 10 men. Projections show that in 1980 there will be 177 women for every 100 men in the age group 85 and over. The percentage of older people in the populations of the individual states ranges from 2 percent to 12.9 percent. In the 1960 census, New York, Pennsylvania and Wisconsin joined the States having 10 percent or more of their population age 65 and over.

As of July 1974, there were approximately 31 million persons 60 years old and over living in the United States. This number is projected to increase to 41 million by the year 2000. Because of increases in longevity in the past several decades and generally low fertility since the 1920's (except for the post-war "baby boom" era), the elderly are becoming an increasing proportion of the nation's population. The demographic characteristics of the elderly, such as age, sex, and race, have been undergoing marked shifts for many years and current projections indicate that these trends will most likely continue to the end of this century. Those segments of the elderly population, such as females (who are often widowed and likely to live alone), blacks, and the very oldest—who suffer most from the commonly cited problems of the aged such as poor health, low income, and social isolation—are the segments which are projected to become an even larger proportion of the elderly than they are today.[5]

Studies further revealed that the financial situation of older people is strongly influenced by their lack of employment income. Only 25 percent of persons 65 and over have income from employment, and often they work only part time. On the other hand, only 5 percent of this age group have no income from employment or public programs. Four out of five receive income from public programs. The old-age survivors and disability insurance program pays benefits to 66 percent of persons 65 and over. A million more are eligible to receive benefits whenever they retire.

Many older people have low incomes. Just exactly how many varies not only with the definition of "low," but also with the system of measurement. Data for individuals must arbitrarily apportion income between husband and wife, and he may be over 65 and she below. Older heads of families may benefit from family income contributed by younger persons. Often excluded are the aged in institutions. By most measurements, however, 50 to 60 percent of the people 65 and over will not have more than $1,000 a year cash income.[6]

Many have some savings and other assets. According to Federal Reserve studies, about half of the older people have no liquid assets or less than $1,000. The most common asset, as well as the one of greatest value, is equity in the home. In some ways too, the financial needs may be reduced for the older person who has retired, whose children are self-supporting and whose house is paid for. His or her resources may be strained, however, by higher than average medical costs. He or she spends nearly twice as much for medical care as the average person in the total population, and is less likely to be protected by health insurance. Generally, older people who have the higher incomes have the additional resources and more adequate insurance. Federal programs for the aging have been estimated to total 17 billion in benefits, services, and income tax savings. In 1960 they amounted to around an average of $900 for each person 65 and over.[7]

Older workers, age 45 and over now make up about 40 percent of the nation's work force. An additional 5.5 million are estimated to be needed to meet the demands of the 1960s. The employment opportunities suggested by this are somewhat offset by two factors. In spite of favorable research evidence regarding his ability, the unemployed older worker often runs up against employer reluctance to hire him. This is reflected in the longer duration of unemployment he experiences, although to the older worker unemployment is not markedly different from that of younger workers.

A second factor is that many of the fastest-growing occupations require new skills and retraining. The individual older worker may not always be in a favorable position to obtain such training. A particular problem may exist for the middle aged woman proposing to re-enter the labor force following the period of heaviest family responsibility. Regardless, projections indicate that she will account for a large portion of the anticipated increase.

The Federal Council on Aging finds older persons tend to maintain their independent living arrangements as long as possible. Two out of three live in their own homes. Others live in someone else's home, usually that of a relative. Only 6 percent are in an institutional environment. There is evidence of new patterns of living. Increasing numbers of middle-aged people are reviewing their goals and planning for their later years. Older people are finding new ways to take advantage of the added hours and free time which become available on retirement. In 1960, there were about 17 million persons 65 and over in the United States, more than 5 times as many as there were in 1900. In the same period the number of middle aged persons (45 to 64) increased from 10 million to 36 million. Persons 65 and over and those 45 to 64 constituted 4 percent and 14 percent respectively, of the total population in 1900. By 1960 these percentages had increased to 9 percent and 20 percent.

Population projections indicate a population 65 and over of 24.5 million in 1970 and a population of 45 to 64 of nearly 44 million. If current levels of fertility persist to 1980, middle-aged and older persons will constitute about the same proportions of the total population as they did in 1960. If fertility declines, however, they will become a larger part of the total.[8]

Figures for 1960 show that women outnumber men by about 5 percent at ages 45-54, but by 46 percent at 85 and over. During this century, this sex differential in mortality has increased and by 1980 there will be about 177 women for every 100 men in the age group 85 and over. One third of men and women 75 and over are married and live in their own household. From ages 45-54 to age 75 and over, the percentage of men and women who are husbands and wives living in their own household decreases from 77 percent to 33 percent. The percentage of persons who are heads of their houshold but have no relatives living with them increases from 6 percent to 20 percent, and the percentage of persons living in the household of others, largely their adult children, increases from 7 percent to 25 percent.[9]

Currently, how many older Americans are there? In 1976, one in every 9 persons in the United States was 65 plus (22.9 million men and women). During 1975, about 1.8 million persons reached the age of 65 and 1.2 million persons 65+ died, a net increase of 555,000 older Americans (1,510 per day). The proportion of the population 65 years old and over varied by race and ethnic origin: 11% for whites, 8% for blacks, and 4% for persons of Spanish origin. Between 1900 and 1976, the percentage of the United States population aged 65 plus more than doubled (4.1% in 1900 and 10.7% in 1976) while the number increased about sevenfold (from 3 million to 23 million). At present death rates, the older population is expected to increase 39% to 32 million by 2000. If the present low birth rate persists, these 32 million will be 12.2% of the total population of about 260 million. If the birth rate should continue to decline, they would represent 12.9% of a total population of about 246 million.

Where do older Americans live in the United States? In 1976, about half (46%) of persons 65+ lived in seven states. California and New York had over 2 million, and Florida, Illinois, Ohio,

Pennsylvania and Texas had over 1 million. Since 1970, the 65+ group in seven states has grown by more than 25%— Nevada (52%), Arizona (46%), Florida (40%), Hawaii (36%), New Mexico (34%), Alaska (32%), and South Carolina (26%).

The 65+ group was 12% or more of the total population in 10 states— Florida (16.4%), Arkansas (13.1%), Iowa (12.8%), Missouri (12.7%), Nebraska (12.6%), Kansas, Rhode Island and South Dakota (12.5%), Oklahoma (12.3%), and Maine (12.0%).

About 31% of the elderly lived outside the nation's metropolitan areas in 1975, compared to 26% of all other age groups.[10]

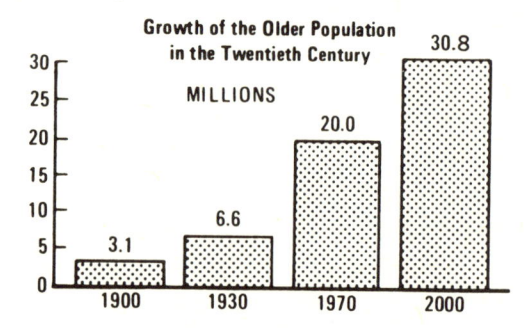

Growth of the Older Population in the Twentieth Century (MILLIONS)

- 1900: 3.1
- 1930: 6.6
- 1970: 20.0
- 2000: 30.8

The Older Population in the Twentieth Century

Year	Number (000's)	% of Total	Men (000's)	Women (000's)	Ratio Women/Men
1900	3,080	4.1	1,555	1,525	98/100
1930	6,634	5.4	3,325	3,309	100/100
1970	19,972	9.8	8,367	11,605	139/100
1976	22,934	10.7	9,364	13,571	145/100
2000	31,822	12.2–12.9	12,717	19,105	150/100

Has life expectancy changed? A child born in 1900 could expect to live an average of about 47 years; a child born in 1975 could expect to live 25 years longer—an average of 72 years. The major part of the increase occurred because of reduced death rates for children and young adults. More people now reach old age, but then do not live much longer than did their ancestors who reached age 65 in 1900.

At age 65, life expectancy is 16 years—14 years for men but 18 years for women. As a result of this sex difference in life expectancy, which begins at birth, there were 145 older women per 100 older men in 1976 and the disparity continued to grow with age. (Assuming that the 1975 death rates do not change in the future, 82% of female children will live to the age of 65 as compared with only 68% for male children.) More than 1.2 million older people died in 1975, a rate of 54 per 1,000—67 for men and 48 for women. The death rate for the under 65 group was 4 per 1,000. Three-fourths of all of the deaths of older persons resulted from heart disease (44%) and cancer (18%).

In 1975, the nation spent approximately 103 billion dollars for personal health care. About 30 billion on 29% of this amount was spent for older persons. The per capita health care cost for an older person was $1,360, nearly three times as much as the $472 spent for younger adults. Benefits from government programs such as Medicare accounted for two-thirds of the health expenditures of older persons, as compared with three-tenths for adults under 65. About 5% or approximately one million older persons lived in institutions of all kinds in 1976. Most older persons lived in a family setting. In the noninstitutional population, the numbers of older men and older women living in a family setting were about the same (7.4 million), but since there are many more older women than older men (145 per 100), the proportion of older men in family settings was 83% and of women 58%.[11]

What is the current marital status of older persons: In 1976, most older men (79%) were married; most older women (53%) were widows. There were more than five times as many widows as widowers. Over one-third (37%) of the older married men had wives under 65 years of age. In 1973 the states (a total of 41 states and the District of Columbia) that participated in the reporting program for marriages reported 16,407 brides and 33,020 grooms aged 65+. These were first marriages for about 5% of both men and women. Most were remarriages of older persons who were previously widowed (85% of the brides and 81% of the grooms).

Proportion of Population Aged 65+: 1976

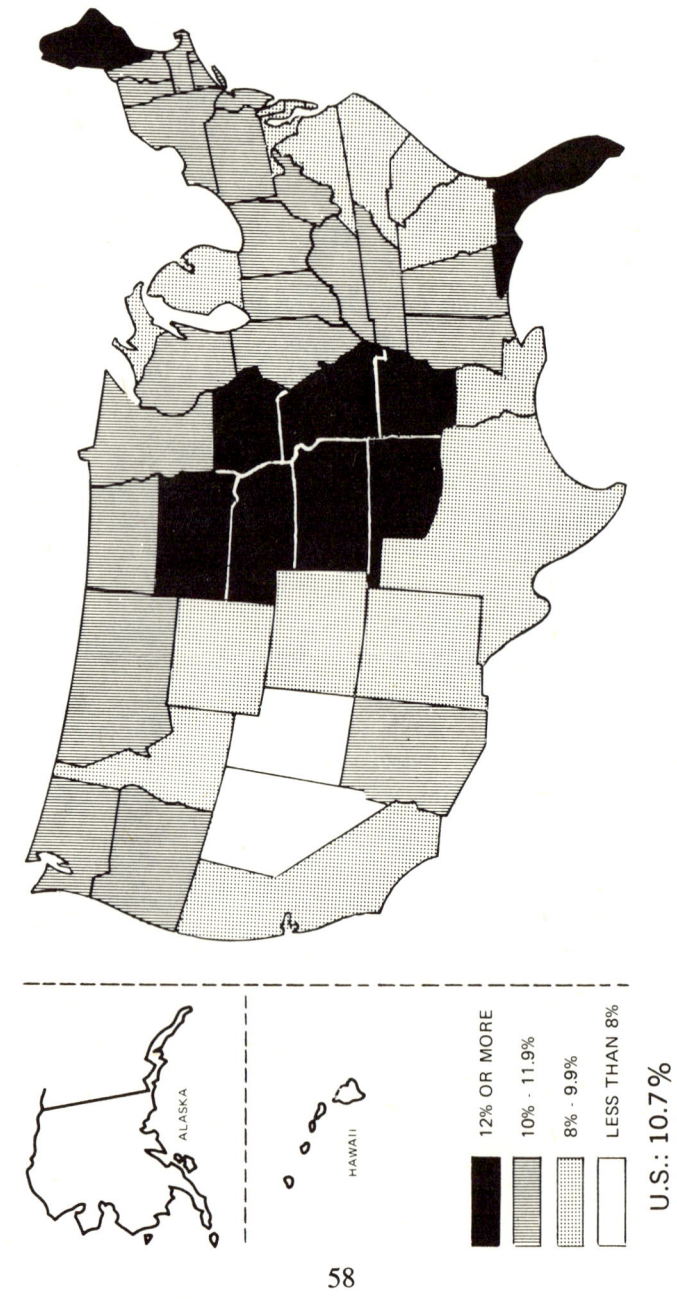

- 12% OR MORE
- 10% - 11.9%
- 8% - 9.9%
- LESS THAN 8%

U.S.: 10.7%

Estimated Population Aged 65+, by State: 1976

State	Number (000's)	Percent of Total Population	Rank[1]	Percent Increase, 1970-1976	State	Number (000's)	Percent of Total Population	Rank[1]	Percent Increase, 1970-1976
Total	23,153	10.6	—	14.9	Nebraska	196	12.6	5	7.2
Excluding Puerto Rico and out-lying areas	22,934	10.7	—	14.8	Nevada	47	7.7	48[t]	51.8
Alabama	388	10.6	25[t]	19.7	New Hampshire	91	11.1	19[t]	16.5
Alaska	9	2.4	54[t]	32.2	New Jersey	787	10.7	23[t]	13.4
Arizona	235	10.4	27[t]	46.2	New Mexico	94	8.0	47	33.9
Arkansas	277	13.1	2	17.2	New York	2,068	11.4	15[t]	6.0
California	2,121	9.9	34	18.4	North Carolina	513	9.4	37	24.5
Colorado	218	8.4	44[t]	16.4	North Dakota	75	11.7	13[t]	12.6
Connecticut	330	10.6	25[t]	14.9	Ohio	1,089	10.2	31[t]	9.6
Delaware	51	8.8	41[t]	17.7	Oklahoma	339	12.3	9	13.7
District of Columbia	72	10.3	30	2.9	Oregon	266	11.4	15[t]	17.9
Florida	1,383	16.4	1	40.4	Pennsylvania	1,404	11.8	11[t]	10.9
Georgia	443	8.9	40	21.3	Rhode Island	116	12.5	6[t]	11.5
Hawaii	60	6.8	50	36.0	South Carolina	240	8.4	44[t]	26.3
Idaho	81	9.7	35	20.7	South Dakota	86	12.5	6[t]	7.6
Illinois	1,171	10.4	27[t]	7.6	Tennessee	453	10.7	23[t]	18.5
Indiana	540	10.2	31[t]	9.9	Texas	1,193	9.6	36	20.8
Iowa	367	12.8	3	5.0	Utah	94	7.7	48[t]	22.4
Kansas	289	12.5	6[t]	8.8	Vermont	53	11.1	19[t]	12.6
Kentucky	373	10.9	22	10.9	Virginia	441	8.8	41[t]	21.0
Louisiana	355	9.2	38[t]	16.2	Washington	374	10.4	27[t]	16.6
Maine	128	12.0	10	11.9	West Virginia	214	11.8	11[t]	10.7
Maryland	350	8.4	44[t]	17.3	Wisconsin	523	11.3	17	11.0
Massachusetts	682	11.7	13[t]	7.6	Wyoming	34	8.7	43	14.0
Michigan	834	9.2	38[t]	11.3	American Samoa	1	2.4	54[t]	4.8
Minnesota	445	11.2	18	9.3	Guam	2	1.9	56	28.4
Mississippi	259	11.0	21	17.2	Puerto Rico	208	6.6	51	17.5
Missouri	608	12.7	4	8.9	Trust Territories	4	3.6	53	30.9
Montana	77	10.2	31[t]	11.7	Virgin Islands	4	3.8	52	61.3

[1] States are ranked in order of decreasing percentages (highest percentage is rank 1, lowest is 56).
[t] Tied in ranking. States with identical percentages receive identical rank number with following rank number(s) skipped to allow for number in tie.

59

One of every seven couples with a husband 65+ received incomes less than $4,000 in 1975. At the other end of the income scale, one of every five elderly couples had incomes of $10,000 or more. The income of elderly persons living alone or with nonrelatives was more skewed to the lower end of the income distribution. Half received incomes under $3,000 while only one of six received more than $6,000.[12]

What kind of life do we see for the older people of tomorrow? What changes in the climate and environment of aging may we expect if the states and communities and the nation, too, show the same interest they have shown in measuring the dimensions of the needs and problems in developing their recommendations? What do we see if we look ahead 10 or 20 years into the future?

The elderly of 1980 may be very different from the elderly of today. Most of today's oldsters were born and received their early training in the 19th century. Those of two decades hence will be products of the 20th century with different values and probably different social characters. Furthermore, the pioneering of today's generation of older people is establishing new patterns and precedents which will be of great value to those of the oncoming generations. One of the assurances derived from the reports of the states is that the later years will be not only longer but more healthy and vigorous too. Older people grown up in the 20th century, with longer exposure to the concepts of positive health, will have developed better habits of nutrition, exercise, and activity, and more compelling awareness of need for periodic checkups to discover latent, insidious conditions. Twenty years hence, research will have yielded much greater knowledge of the processes of aging, and of chronic diseases. All manner of personnel, professionally trained within their fields but with specialized knowledge of aging, will be providing services through a vast network of health education programs.

There will be geriatric diagnostic centers which will take the total person and his circumstances into account, treatment

Percent Distribution by Income: 1975

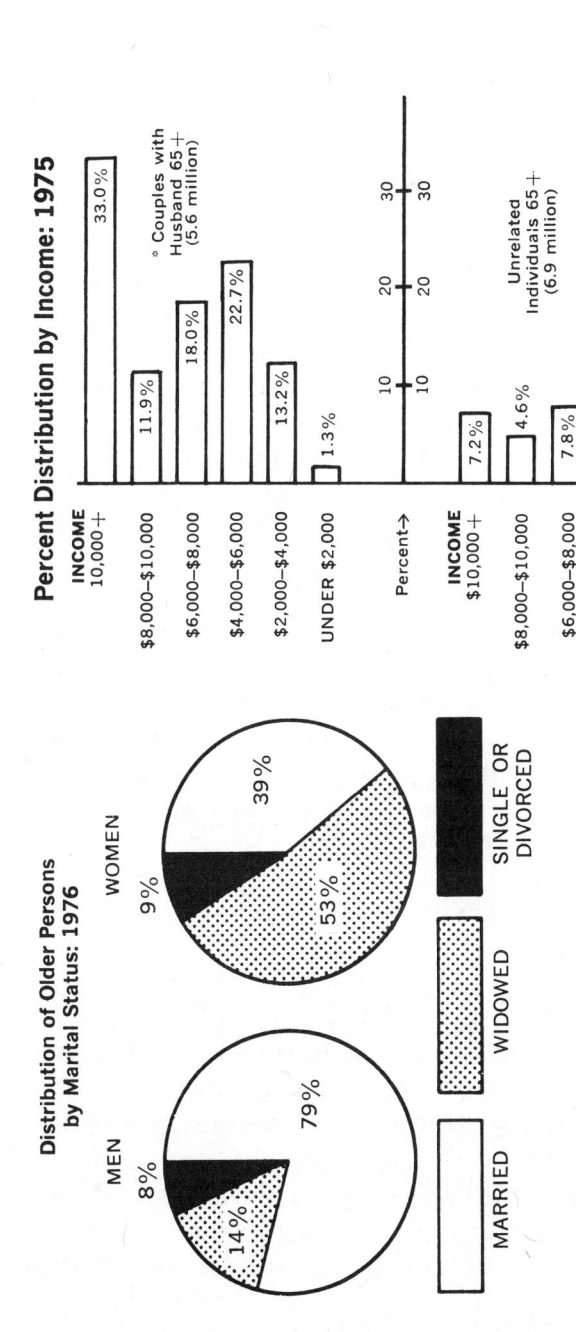

Couples with Husband 65+ (5.6 million)*

INCOME	Percent
$10,000+	33.0%
$8,000–$10,000	11.9%
$6,000–$8,000	18.0%
$4,000–$6,000	22.7%
$2,000–$4,000	13.2%
UNDER $2,000	1.3%

Unrelated Individuals 65+ (6.9 million)

INCOME	Percent
$10,000+	7.2%
$8,000–$10,000	4.6%
$6,000–$8,000	7.8%
$4,000–$6,000	18.3%
$3,000–$4,000	20.3%
$2,000–$3,000	28.6%
UNDER $2,000	13.2%

* For couples, data are restricted to 2-person families in order to exclude income received by other family members in larger families.

Distribution of Older Persons by Marital Status: 1976

MEN
- Married: 79%
- Widowed: 14%
- Single or Divorced: 8%

WOMEN
- Married: 39%
- Widowed: 53%
- Single or Divorced: 9%

facilities which embody the restorative techniques being evolved in the pilot programs of today. Most of the suffering and early death from heart and circulatory diseases and from cancer will have been prevented, and few will experience the agonizing pains of arthritis and rheumatism.

If the aspirations of the states are realized, most older people in the 1980's will enjoy incomes geared to the levels of their needs and styles of life.

One of the greatest changes to be noted by the 1980's will be in the attitude toward retirement. In our economy of increasing energy, automation and abundance, retirement earned after a specified period in the work force and determined by the total volume of goods and services required will be an accepted and common expectation of all who desire it. Most will have had systematic preparation for retirement and many will taper off their work careers through gradual retirement arrangements. Part-time work opportunities will be far more numerous for retirees who wish to keep a hand in work and for mature women whose household duties or other interests prevent their working full time. Older people in the 1980's will be engaged in a variety of leisure pursuits. Many more will be in schools and colleges as the schools come to recognize the desire of older people to pursue intellectual interests and keep abreast of the times. Reading, the arts, crafts, contemplation, serving on advisory boards will be some of the activities of this subculture.

In the report of progress and goals, the Conference on Aging in 1961 clearly saw that "perhaps within a decade, general recognition of the nature and potentialities of the later stages of life and increased awareness by older people of their community of interests in the population, will have led them to develop a subculture of their own. Several of the States have already noted the tendency of older people to seek out their peers and often to create their own organizations for sharing experiences. Members of the subculture may be expected to place increasingly higher values on leisure and freedom of movement, to show greater concern for protecting the purchasing power of retirement incomes, to seek expansion of facilities and services through which their particular needs can be met, and to show an increasing desire to serve as their own interpreters of their needs and styles of life. Positive life styles in later maturity and old age will be widely recognized. A variety of images of successful aging will have replaced today's stereotypes associated with dependency, deterioration and complete withdrawal."[13]

The Search for Alternatives

Government projections for the eighties have lulled us into feeling the social and financial needs of the elderly will be adequately met. Actually this is not entirely the case. A most important variable has been left out. Consider the highly significant and general indifference in our society toward older people. It is plainly visible in daily interaction. Western society is "youth oriented;" we reflect this in our behavioral patterns and attitudes. Older people do not receive the "stande" and deference due them. They are discriminated against in industry. The factory worker, the white collar worker, middle managers, and even the professional, are taught to feel early in the game they are expendable, to be replaced in the marketplace.

Robert MacIver has said that "we cannot dismiss this type of investigation from our reckoning and that probably it excites more interest than any other kind."[14]

Existing attitudes today are ambivalent. The Federal Government through the Department of Health, Education and Welfare is attempting through pilot programs to meet the needs of the elderly. On the other hand, many in the private sector encourage social isolation, hold out inducements and recommend "ideal living" for retired or older people in homes, complexes or apartment living that cater exclusively to the older citizens. There has been criticism of this type of living with the reminder of the social value of diversity and the benefits to be derived from all kinds and all ages of people living together.

Post-industrial society has ushered in a significant cohort of older men and women in a steadily increasing population. They are healthier, live longer, are better educated, more independent and enjoy new life styles. The Civil Rights Movement and the Women's Movement have touched this sector too. They are becoming better organized and are making greater demands on government. No longer will they accept discrimination in terms of how long they can work or settle for the limits set on how much they can earn and still be eligible to receive social security payments. They are also outspoken in their criticism of the Federal Government's delay in establishing a comprehensive National Health Insurance Program. Legislators are beginning to listen to them because they represent a large and growing voting population with developing clout.

What we must face up to is the need for an updated approach to the expanding area of Gerontology, that it is very complex and that it invites a whole new way of looking at meeting the needs of the older members of our society. Perhaps a beginning in establishing a new value system would lie in attaching greater social value to the elderly by extending to them respect and appreciation for their past efforts and by recognizing them as a viable force still capable of making a contribution to the society. There is need for establishing a Department of Gerontology to handle research, health care, make social policy, in addition to initiating pilot programs. The importance and complexity of this area and expanding population justifies the creating of such a Department.

The Federal Government through such a Department and through its social policy implemented and carried out in cooperation with both state and local efforts can do much towards raising the depreciated social value of this subculture. Criticism is also directed to the state level where legislators should recognize they represent not a partial constituency but a population which includes older citizens as well who are being short-changed. What better evidence than the fact that in some areas they are not receiving a census count by the school districts. Why should it be necessary for an amendment to come up on the floor three times in Albany in regard to a census of citizens over 60 by the school districts?

Increasing recognition by the elderly that they do have clout and the appearance of lobbying groups in their behalf are convincing both state legislators as well as Congressman to take a "harder" look at our older citizens and to become more responsive to their demands. Attitudes will have to change and the infrastructure expanded to meet the specialized and complex needs of Gerontology. How we respond to these challenges are among the more important issues on the agenda!

BIBLIOGRAPHY

Aging in the States. *White House Conference on Aging*, 1961.

MacIver, Robert. *Social Causation*, Harper & Row, New York, 1964.

Nevins, Allan. Saturday Review, "*The Explosive Excitement of History*," April 6, 1968.

Sanders, Marion K. Harper's, "*The Sex Crusaders from Missouri*," May, 1968.

U.S. Department of Health, Education and Welfare. *Estimates of Size and Characteristics of the Older Population in 1974 and Projections to the year 2000*, May 1975.

HEW Office of Human Development, Administration on Aging.
—— Facts About Older Americans, 1977.

White House Conference on Aging—Federal Council on Aging, 1961.

Whyte, William H. *Street Corner Society*, University of Chicago Press, 1943.

FOOTNOTES

[1] Allan Nevins, *Saturday Review*. "The Explosive Excitement of History," April 6, 1968.

[2] Marion K. Sanders, "The Sex Crusaders from Missouri," Harper's, May 1968, p. 48-9.

[3] William H. Whyte, *Street Corner Society*, University of Chicago Press, 1943, p. 318.

[4] White House Conference on Aging 1961, Federal Council on Aging, 4.

[5] U.S. Dept. of Health, Education & Welfare, Statistical Memo No. 13. "Estimates of the Size and Characteristics of the Older Population in 1974 and Projections to the Year 2000," May 1975, 8.

[6] White House Conference on Aging Report 1961, 5.

[7] *Ibid.*, 5.
[8] *Ibid.*, 8.
[9] *Ibid.*, 9.
[10] U.S. Department of Health, Education, and Welfare, Office of Human Development, Administration on Aging, National Clearing House on Aging, "Facts about Older Americans 1977," Publ. 77-220006. Statistics and charts on pp. 56, 58, 59 and 61 from same source.
[11] *Ibid.*
[12] *Ibid.*
[13] White Conference on Aging Report, 1961, p. 164-165.
[14] MacIver, Robert. *Social Causation*, New York: Harper & Row, 1964, 150.

23 Jews from Recife:

Attitudes & Prejudices in New Amsterdam

Who was the early American Jew? What brought him to the American shore in the mid-seventeenth century? How did the new environment influence his inner self, religious outlet, goals? What was the attitude of the other members of the New Amsterdam colony, both officials and townspeople, towards them? What manner of life and community did they build here?

The colonial Jew who had to face the Indians, endure the hazards of the frontier life was not the same man who rocked back and forth, intoning the Talmud. A new Jew was being created.

Early American Jewish life in its formative stage is best seen according to Jacob Rader Marcus, Professor of Jewish History of Hebrew Union College in Cincinnati, as covering the years 1649 to about 1790, which is part of the Sephardic period. The Sephardim or Spanish-Portuguese Jews, the first settlers here, ceased to be the majority group in this country no later than the first quarter of the eighteenth century, but their religious culture and synagogue discipline, which were accepted by those who followed them, were dominant in the American Jewish community until at least the third decade of the nineteenth century. The Sephardic period ended by 1840. This was the last year that Sephardic communal leadership was apparent. Although by that time individuals of Ashkenazic or

German and Polish origin constituted the vast majority of Jews here, the Sephardic congregation, because of their age, wealth, and social prestige, maintained their leadership. They were outstanding among those who aroused American citizens, both Jews and non-Jews, to protest the barbarities inflicted upon innocent Jews in Damascus in 1840. They were in the vanguard in this, the first concerted act of a newborn American Jewry.[1]

Seventeenth century Sephardim whose influence was significant in the early Jewish colony included Uriel da Costa, an early deist, Isaac Aboab, who became the first Rabbi in America (in Pernambuco), and Manasseh ben Israel, printer, author and scholar. It was Manasseh ben Israel who conferred with Oliver Cromwell in England personally for two years from 1655 to 1657 for the readmission of the Jews to England. Coming at a time of expansion for England with colonies already in North America, Cromwell was receptive to this request because it was useful to his purposes of annexing all of Spain's empire in America.[2]

Nathan Glazer feels we may get a much better understanding of the early Jewish settlement in New Amsterdam in 1654 by seeing it in the perspective of the Middle Ages than in the perspective of later American history. Under the heavy heel of the (Spanish) Inquisition the Jewish community was expelled from Spain and later around 1497 from Portugal. This religious persecution followed them as exiles even in South America. During medieval times in Spain the Jews had their Golden Age. Because of the tolerance of the Moslem Moorish rulers, they became doctors, lawyers, teachers, mathematicians, poets, philosophers and merchant princes. When Spain drove the Moors out the Jews were also victims. Cities were massacred; Jews were given the choice of conversion or death. Those who intermarried or converted were called marranos or conversos. Some fled to Portugal, Turkey, Poland and Holland. Others went to Brazil in the early sixteenth century and even there the Inquisition followed them.[3] The New Christians or Marranos, as the Jews forced into an outward acceptance of Christianity were called, frequently followed the trade routes along the Mediterranean Sea to Venice, Naples, the Levant and Egypt. At first only individual New Christians found their way to Antwerp. With the winning of Dutch independence the union of the northern provinces of Netherland proclaimed at Utrecht in 1579 guaranteed freedom of conscience to the people of Netherland.

That charter of religious liberty and the crippling of the Spanish sea power in 1588 marked the beginning of the active movement of the Iberian Jews to Holland. This period also found Portugal, Holland and England vying for new markets in the New World. As a result of the Chmielnicki uprising in Poland where Jews suffered heavily, Jewish immigration reversed westward to mercantile cities where Jews settled in Holland and North Germany. Here they found Jews of Spanish origin who had settled in Amsterdam, no longer as New Christians, but openly recognized as Jews. The Portuguese Jewish community of Amsterdam grew rapidly in numbers and importance. From Holland, many also went to Brazil, Surinam, Curacao. A number of them engaged in international exchange and import-export commerce. What is not generally recognized is that the period of the great development of international sea-borne commerce in the large centers such as Antwerp, Amsterdam and Hamburg coincides with the period of the greatest activity of the Sephardim in those centers. King Christian IV of Denmark seeing Hamburg's ocean trade grow so much through the enterprise of its Sephardic merchants wrote to the head of the Sephardic community in Amsterdam to invite the Sephardic merchants to settle in Gluckstadt under guarantee of full freedom and rights.[4]

When the refugees from Spain and Portugal arrived in Holland in 1593, they worshipped secretly in a private home. Four years later at a Yom Kippur service, they were attacked by suspicious citizens who mistook them for Catholics. When they explained they were secret Jews the council granted them permission to remain. In 1598 a synagogue was publicly dedicated. More Marranos came. By the early seventeenth century Holland became known as the Dutch Jerusalem. There were more than 500 Jewish families, most of them wealthy, enterprising, and highly cultured. The Jews became interested in oceanic trade and their capital helped to build up both the Dutch East and Dutch West India Companies.[5]

Shareholders of the Dutch West Indies Co.

Shareholders of the Dutch West Indies Co. were divided into two classes, chief shareholders (Hooflparticipanten) and minor shareholders (minder participanten). The names of the Jewish chief stockholders for the years 1654 and 1655 are not accessible. Those for 1656 and 1658 which probably contain those for 1655 and 1654 include: 1656 Abram Isaac Perera, Area Crist of Nunes, Abram Isaac Bueno, Bento Osoric, Josep D'Acosta, Louys Rodriguez de Sousa, Ferdinando dios de Britto. A further list of April 1658 includes Francisco Vaz de Granto, Francisco Lopo Henriques, Alvarez Naugera, Josepho de los Rios, Ruy Gommes Frontiera, Aron Chomes Vaz, Diones Jennis, Diego Vaz de Sousa.

Joseph d'Acosta, whose name appears as one of the principal shareholders, is no doubt identical with the one of that name who came to New Amsterdam in August 1655, when he appears for the first time in the records in a suit against the owner of the Spotted Cow for damages to his goods. He is the same Joseph D'Acosta of Amsterdam who is the brother of the celebrated Uriel D'Acosta. The records indicate he leased a house in December 1655 in New Amsterdam from Michael de Comeman for one year at an annual rental of 250 guilders. He apparently was not here in July 1655 when the Jews petitioned for the purchase of a burying ground, as his name was not signed to that petition.[6]

Who Were the Marranos?

The Marranos were New Christians or secret Jews who had accepted Christianity only to escape death and remained at heart completely Jewish. Outwardly they lived as Christians. They took their children to church to be baptized, though they washed off the traces of the ceremony as soon as they returned home. They would go to the priest to be married, and in the privacy of their houses performed another ceremony. Behind this outward sham they remained at heart Jews as they had always been. They kept all the traditional ceremonies, observed the Sabbath as far as they could. Some would eat meat prepared in the Jewish fashion. Many had their children circumcised. They married amongst themselves for the most part. They would form religious associations with titularly Catholic objects and under the patronage of some Christian saint, using this as a cover for observing their ancestral rites. In belief and largely in practice, they remained Jews in all but name. They were moreover able to transmit their disbelief to their children, who though born in the dominant faith and baptized at birth, were as little sincere in their attachment to it as their fathers.[7]

How the Marranos and Other Jews Were Treated in Holland

The Marranos as well as other Jews fleeing from Poland were not admitted to civil and religious equality. They did win freedom to worship publicly. They could not engage in handicrafts or engage in trade. Within the scope of these limitations, they prospered as a group and it can be said the commercial skill and connections of the Jews in Holland played an important part in making Holland one of the great powers of Europe at that time.[8] It should also be noted that it was to the Directors of the Dutch West Indies Company, many of whom were influential shareholders, that the early Jewish colonists of New Amsterdam looked to for support in their fight to remain and fight for religious freedom.

The Marranos in Brazil

When the Dutch captured Recife in 1630 the local Marranos threw off their disguise. Two Jews, Nuno Alvarez Franco and Manuel Fernandez Drago, planned the capture, which was an armed expedition sent out by the Dutch West India Company. The Dutch themselves, in forming the West India Company in 1622 in furtherance of the scheme of conquest, counted upon the support of the native New Christians, while the fugitives in Holland invested in the shares. It was therefore natural that in those places which were captured by the Dutch the Marranos seized the first opportunity to declare their true identity.

What kind of life did the Jews lead in Recife? It was a vigorous life, and it was a religious life. They had their own synagogues and their own rabbis; one was Isaac Aboab de Fonseca, the first American Rabbi, born of New Christian parentage at Castrodaire in Portugal, and Ralphael Moses de Aguilar, who acted as reader or Hazzan. As for occupations, most were merchants. A few were professional men, engineers, and there was a practicing lawyer, Michael Cordoso, the first Jewish attorney in the Western world. Jews owned large sugar plantations, they cultivated tobacco. They exported Brazilian dyewood. In addition to the merchant and the financier, there developed the farmer and the artisan. There was also a transoceanic trade in marmalade and wheat, in salted meats, felt hats and sugar. There grew up dynamic cultural patterns whose activities centered around the "esnoga," as the synagogue was popularly called. The marrying, the feasting, the mourning and the fasting were centered there. Group discipline and group folkways stemmed from the religious life of the transplanted communities. It was the social agency through which the Jews met the impact of life in a new setting and through which it imposed the attitudes Jews were expected to adopt toward the government and their Christian neighbors.[9]

In the two sieges of Recife where Jews fought desperately with the Dutch against the Portuguese, many died and Aboab recorded the tribulations through which they had passed in a lengthy Hebrew poem—the first specimen of Jewish literature to be composed in America. Following the second siege, the city was forced to capitulate in 1654 to the Portuguese. The Jewish population in Recife at that time was 5,000; they were given three months to get out. The reconquest of Brazil by the Portuguese and the consequent breakup of the local communities of Marranos who returned to Judaism under Dutch protection is viewed as an episode of the highest importance in Jewish history.[10]

The First Jewish Settlement
The "Jewish Pilgrims" September 1654

Not all Recife Jews went back to Holland. The surrender of 1654 created the Dutch Colonial Jewish Diaspora—some Jews went to French Martinique and Guadeloupe, others to Jamaica and English Barbados.[11] In September 1654, 23 people of the approximately 150 Jewish families who had left Brazil arrived in New Amsterdam. Their arrival is recorded in the oldest extant volume in manuscript form of the New York City Record as the minutes of the Burgomasters and Schepens of New Amsterdam from 1653 to 1654, with the ordinances of New Amsterdam from 1657 to 1661, and is first mentioned in a record of the meeting dated September 7, 1654. This volume is to be found at the City Clerk's Office in the Municipal Building in New York City. The record states:

> "Jacques de la Motte, captain of the bark St. Cathrien, requests by a petition the payment for the freight and food of the Jews brought here from Cape St. Anthony, according to agreement and contract by which each is individually bound; and that therefore the furniture and whatever else the Jews have aboard his bark may be publicly sold by order of the Court towards the payment of their debt. It was orally de-

clared that the Netherlanders who came over with them, are not included in the contract and have satisfied him.

Salomon Pietersz, a Jew, appeared in Court and said that nine hundred and odd guilders of the 2500 florins have been paid and that there are 23 souls, big as well as little, who must pay equally. The petition and the contract having been seen by the noble Court, it is decreed that, according to the contract, the Jews shall pay that which remains of their debt within twice 24 hours after date, and meanwhile the furniture and whatever else is in the hands of the petitioner should remain as security without alienating the same."[12]

To collect the balance of the passage money, the property of the Jews was sold at auction. Three adults were imprisoned for the passage debts but they were released promising the captain to get financial help from their kin in Holland. Asser Levy, one of the adults imprisoned, later became a leader in the Jewish community in the fight for equality.[13] He was one of the first Jews to own property on Long Island; his son's family settled in the Hamptons.[14]

Jacob Rader Marcus said: "No Jew is ever the first in any town; there is always one who had been there before him." Actually, Jacob Barsiman, the first Jewish settler, arrived August 22, 1654 under passport of a party of emigrants from Holland on the ship Peartree sent by the Dutch West India Company to populate its new colony. He cleared land, traded with the Indians and for a time hired out as manual labor. He was responsible for the first case in which observance of the Jewish Sabbath was officially recognized as a valid reason for failing to answer a court summons. "Though the defendant is absent yet no default is entered against him as he was summoned on his Sabbath."[15]

The Records of the Burgomaster also give the name of Salomon Pieterson who had arrived some time in the summer of 1654 to do business in the colony. Barsiman and Pieterson interceded on behalf of the 23 refugees from Brazil.[16] Anita Libman Leveson calls attention to the fact that when the Peartree brought Jacob Barsiman to New Amsterdam there were scattered Jewish settlers along the north Atlantic seaboard. But the group from Brazil was the first to migrate as a unit composed of families,[17] and they also established the first organized Jewish Community in that region.[18] Peter Stuyvesant who was the governor of the colony of New Amsterdam was opposed to the band of Jews and wrote to the Directors in Holland in the hope he might be permitted to expel them. Stuyvesant also requested "that none of the Jewish nation be permitted to invade New Netherlands."[19] In describing the New Amsterdam climate when the Jews from Recife landed here, Abram Voss Goodman states that "Stuyvesant was an implacable governor, a bitter clergy fiercely opposing every faith except the Dutch Reformed Church, in addition to a population bigoted and suspicious of Jews."[20]

Along with Salomon Pieterson, Barsiman interceded on behalf of the 23 refugees. These protests were sent to the representatives of the Jews in Amsterdam who were mainly Portuguese Jews. They stated they understood obstacles were being placed against the issuance of permits or passports to Jews to go to New Netherlands. Attention was called to the fact that the Dutch West Indies Company had by general resolution consented to allow all those who wished to emigrate to be permitted, and that since Holland Jews had resided there for many years enjoying being burghers or citizens, why should they be excepted from the privilege of emigrating? The directors overruled Stuyvesant and under an order of February 15, 1655 Jews were allowed to travel to, live in, and trade to and in the colony of New Amsterdam.[21]

After Stuyvesant's objections were overruled, a number of Jews went to New Amsterdam from Holland under regularly issued passports. There is also a letter written by Domini Johannes Megapolenses, the Dutch Minister in New Netherlands to his superiors, the Classis of Amsterdam, dated March 18, 1655 expressing his apprehension in regard to Jewish emigration, particularly concerning the Jews who had arrived early in 1655 after they were given permission for their settlement here with the possibility of many more Jews to follow and build a synagogue. Oppenheim believes the removal of the obstacles to the issuance of these passports and the talk by new arrivals in New Amsterdam of building a synagogue showed a definite plan formed for the extensive emigration of Jews from Holland.[22] It was at this time when the passport was issued to Barsiman that efforts were at the same time being made by Dutch Jews and their celebrated Rabbi Menasseh ben Israel to obtain permission from Cromwell for the resettlement of Jews in England from which they had been excluded since 1290. The Jews between 1630 and 1654 in Brazil had been treated under Dutch rule on an equal basis with other inhabitants, but when the Portuguese took over, they were no longer welcome and sought asylum elsewhere. Oppenheim maintains that the unfriendly treatment received by the first Jews in New Amsterdam hastened the early resettlement of Jews in England.[23]

Leon Huhner writes that the Dutch who settled New Amsterdam were as a body fair-minded and just, yet not a few among them looked upon the arrival of Jews in the colony with open hostility. The Jews of early New York had to fight their way to respect against deep-rooted prejudice and bigotry. A principal reason the Jews were permitted to remain was that Jews in Holland were heavy stockholders in the Dutch West India Company.[24] Tolerated but never really accepted in New Amsterdam, the Jews remained a tiny handful.[25]

In the Dutch period, the Jews were required by law to live in a separate section of the city. There is evidence to indicate this neighborhood was on Whitehall Street near the tip of Manhattan Island. When the British took the city in 1664, the Jews moved closer to one another mainly because of their desire to be near their synagogue and other members of their faith.[26]

Social Structure: The Synagogue Community

The social structure of the New Amsterdam Jewish community can best be viewed in the perspective of the Middle Ages and the Renaissance Jews when they considered themselves and were considered by others to be a nation in exile. While subject to many painful forms of discrimination and persecution, they were still free to be governed by their own law. The Jewish community, not the Jew as an individual, was recognized. With the establishment of the nation state, Jews were expected to assume all political obligations and conform to the cultural pattern of the country of residence as the price of emancipation from ghetto and medieval restrictions. Glazer again cautions us to try to understand the early colonial Jews from the perspective of the seventeenth and not the twentieth century. From that perspective we must see the synagogue not as an independent institution to take care of the religious needs of people but rather as the expression of a unified Jewish community. The Jews of Europe of that period were organized into Kahals or communities recognized and exploited by the sovereign, but they still possessed certain rights of self-government. The community leaders managed the synagogue and appointed a communal rabbi who was an official, not of the synagogue, but of the community. The rabbi determined questions of religious law, arranged for the baking of matzoh, and for the ritually correct slaughter of animals for meat. The synagogue, which in Europe was only one agency of the Jewish community, in New Amsterdam became the community. Contrasted with the Jewish communities in Europe, the Jewish communities in America had no taxing power and could not call on the state authority to enforce their decision.[27] But even without such powers, the synagogue acted like a true community and did have certain disciplinary power over the Jews. For example, the congregation had a monopoly of religious rites; they controlled the cemeteries. In all their wanderings, the Jews have looked upon the synagogue and the "house of life," or burial ground, as the two essentials for their collective life: they transformed an aggregation into a community. Ten months after their arrival in New Amsterdam the Jews petitioned for the right to purchase a burial plot. The request was turned down because they were told there was no need. They obtained a plot a year later; the need had arisen.[28] Glazer stresses that more than social pressure and control of the cemetery was the fact that the idea of the community was then so universal in Jewish life that most Jews simply could not imagine living apart from it. The Jew could not conceive of himself as totally separated from the group.[29]

In broad historical and sociological perspective, therefore, the organization and institutional concept of the idea of community in the first New Amsterdam, later New York Jewish settlement can be depicted in terms of the "synagogue community." All activity centered in and around the synagogue which was the primary institution and the integrating force for the Jews in the locality. The synagogue was the community; within it was the center of education, social, religious and charitable activities. The cemetery served as the permanent geographic nuclear unit of community organization.[30] In July 1655 the Jews of New Amsterdam in a petition to Governor Stuyvesant asked for a tiny piece of land not far from the Battery. "It was initiated by Abraham de Lucena, Salvador Dandrado and Jacob Cohen who sent a petition to be permitted to purchase a burying place for their nation, as they did not wish to bury their dead in the common burying ground."[31]

New arrivals as well as the "poor" were cared for by the synagogue. The awareness that "all Israel is responsible for one another has its roots in the Old World and the reasons why the Jews should care for their own were both religious, social and political as well. All during the colonial period, the members of the congregation assumed this duty. For instance, in the report of the synagogue's expenses in 1729, there is the item "For obras Pias to the poor of this city and outside, and for sending persons to their destination £53.4.1." The Jewish community never turned to the municipal authorities for assistance in taking care of their needy. Rather they looked upon it not only as a duty, but took pride in and considered it a privilege to help fellow Jews in need.[32]

Where a dozen or more Jewish families settled, the first institution to be established in every instance was the synagogue. The "synagogue" as the social structure of the pioneer Jewish settlement can be seen as the first Jewish institutionalized organization, which was a "collective concern."[33] Isaac Franck describes their early collective experiences as "containing in microcosm a number of the same ingredients we find today in an organized local Jewish community."[34] It entailed, for the 23 refugee Jews from Recife, the concerted effort of this small group to enlist the support of fellow Jews in the Dutch West Indies Company in Amsterdam to overcome the resistance of Stuyvesant and his Council to their remaining in the New Amsterdam colony. It was succeeded by a similar group struggle pitted against Stuyvesant for a place for public worship, once again for burial grounds to bury their dead, and repetitiously struggling on in terms of the group effort, always reinforced by their fellow Jews in Amsterdam, to secure for themselves the basic equal rights of citizenship and opportunity extended to others in the colony. In successively winning these civil rights, therefore, the Jewish group made it possible for groups other than the preferred and accepted members of the Dutch Reformed Church to secure their civil rights. In a sense, it can be seen as the unfolding of pluralism in a microcosm in the American political fabric.

The social arm of the synagogue extended to providing free burial where needed and also providing money for matzoh for the Passover Holidays for those who could not afford it. The Ladies Aid group of the synagogue looked after the wants of the needy or new arrivals, and provided where needed for these families food, clothing and coal. The principle of "hakhnassat orhim" provided temporary shelter for newly arrived families. The synagogue offered the "gemilat hasadim," a little financial help to get the family started towards independence.[35]

Education: In traditional Jewish manner, great attention was devoted to the education of the young. Leveson writes that for them "the school was the core of society." The early Jewish school was similar to the early American colonial schools which were conducted entirely under religious auspices. The curriculum was at first confined to the Hebrew language, but later Spanish, English, writing and arithmetic were added. The first Jewish school in America, the New York Yeshivat Minhat Areb, was founded in 1731, shortly after the establishment of the first synagogue in New York 1729, the Mill Street Synagogue. In 1762 Spanish was dropped from the curriculum and the school was called a "publick school." It functioned as a parochial school and considered itself part of the Common School System. It even received a subsidy from the city of New York but these financial grants ceased in 1825 when the Common Council of New York ordered that the Common School Fund no longer be distributed to any religious society.[36]

The laying of a cornerstone and the consecration of a synagogue were important social occasions in the community. Both Jews and Christians attended in large numbers. Besides their intrinsic interest Grinstein writes "these events soon developed an order and form that made them significant important events to witness." Between 1729 and 1860 there were four Spanish and Portuguese dedications. Between 1840 and 1860 a consecration took place in New York on the average of once a year.

There is little information on the dedication of Shearith Israel's Mill Street Synagogue (1729). The four corner foundation stones were sold to the highest bidders and were laid on Thursday, September 8, 1729 between 3:00 and 4:00 P.M. Grinstein also points out in the early days when there was one synagogue in New York, the burial grounds were considered the common property of all the Jews of the city. Those who had absented themselves from the synagogue and had refused to contribute to the maintenance of the synagogue during their lives were refused burial until their heirs had paid a nominal sum for the privilege.[37]

What's Important Is a Minyan

When the English took over the New Amsterdam colony in 1664, renaming it New York, they too like the Dutch shunned the petitions presented by the Jews for the right to build a synagogue. The Jews got together in private homes or even under trees. What was important was that they have a minyan—the ten adult male Jews of any locality coming together in one place comprise all that Judaism says is necessary for public worship. Under the laws of Judaism, the ten men can meet in a field, under a tree, in a home. Members of Shearith Israel began gathering for prayers in an old grist mill, formerly used by the Dutch as a church, which they rented for £8 a year from a Dutch shoemaker in a 1½ story house on Beaver Street between Broadway and Broad Street. At that time there were 855 families in New York, only 25 of them, less than 2 per cent, were Jewish.[38]

£50 Plus Cordwood and Matzoh

The first paid official at Shearith Israel was Saul Pardo, a merchant who had been admitted to burgher rights in 1685. His title was hazzan. In early colonial days, because there were no rabbis, the hazzan took on traditional importance. At first there were volunteers serving without compensation; they were exempt from military service. For reading the services he was paid £50 a year and given 6 cords firewood and enough matzoh for his entire family. A salary of £16 a year plus wood and matzoh was paid to the Shammas who assisted the hazzan, kept the rented quarters clean and saw that candles were always on hand. Leadership in this and in early Jewish communities was vested in a board of officers known as the Junta, a standing committee headed by a president or parnas who kept the synagogue records, maintained the discipline, imposed fines, and awarded honors. Shearith Israel's first president was Luis Gomez, merchant.[39]

For £100, One Loaf of Sugar, One Pound of Tea

In 1729 Congregation Shearith Israel bought a piece of land on Mill Street, not far from their rented quarters. They paid £100, One Loaf of Sugar and One Pound of Tea. Because the law did not permit a Jewish religious body to own property, the lot was purchased in the name of four individuals. Contributions came from all parts of the world. Amsterdam, Holland sent funds; the Chief Rabbi of Curacao sent 264 pieces of eight. However, the majority of contributions for the building came from the Jews of New York. The building was completed in 1730.[40]

How the Jews of New Amsterdam felt about Non Jews

Evidence indicates that the New Amsterdam Jews supported generously non-Jewish movements. For example, in 1671, Asser Levy, one of the leaders in the community, advanced money to the Lutherans to help them build their first church. In 1711 De Lucena and 6 other New York Jews contributed to the fund for the completion of Trinity Church steeple. Robert St. Johns calls attention to the fact that while anti-Jewish feeling was alive, yet in the small New Amsterdam/New York colony "men of one religion were helping men of another to build religious structures." Perhaps the financial help by De Lucena and others also indicated that the New York Jews had become a little more secure in their own civil rights and that they could also be helpful to other groups.[41]

Synagogue Financing

The synagogues of New York were supported mainly by the sale or yearly rental of seats and by voluntary contributions. There were other, minor sources of income. There were admission fees on becoming a member, fees for marriage and burial at many of the synagogues, as well as fines and tuition fees. Tuition fees were used only for educational expenditures; fines, imposed on members or on trustees for various infractions of the rules, were negligible.

Attempts were made from time to time to depart from this system of raising funds. Many advocated the abolition of the offerings; others wanted a return to the old system of taxation existing in Europe and termed "erekh." But for the most part the synagogues retained the sale of seats and the offerings as their main methods of raising funds.

Until 1728, Shearith Israel apparently relied only on offerings and on the sale of mitzvot. But in that year, part of the source was dropped in favor of a tax on men's seats. By 1737 each person affiliated with the congregation was expected to contribute at least forty shillings during the year, otherwise no honors or privileges would be granted him.[42]

Based on the number of seats in the synagogues, on other data, and on other estimates the Jewish population of New York City was:

Year	Number of Jews in New York	Gen. Pop. of City (in round numbers)	Percentage[43]
1695	100	4,000	2.5
1750	300	13,000	2.3

Twenty families are indicated as residing in New York in 1695. These twenty families, considered in very conservative fashion according to Grinstein as consisting of five members to a family, would give a round number of 100. Oppenheim confirms this further in a list which he drew up of some twenty-one families in 1695.[44] The figure of 300 Jews in 1750 is based upon sixty-one seats assigned at Shearith Israel in that year, and again using the multiple of five for each family, Grinstein comes to an approximate number of 300.[45]

The list of hazzanim holding office at temple Shearith Israel include:[46]

	Term
Saul Brown	?-1682
Abraham Haim de Lucena	?-1720
Benjamin Wolf	?
Moses Lopez de Fonseca	1728-1736
David Mendes Machado	1737-1746
Benjamin Pereira	1748-1756

Anti-Jewish Attitudes: Rejection

Marcus writes that "it is a tangled skein that must be unraveled to survey relations between Christians and Jews in colonial America. The threads are not at all monochromatic, and if rejection and hostility are to be found, there is also no lack of acceptance and collaboration."[47]

Only the Dutch Protestants were really welcome in New Amsterdam. Pleading against extending rights to the Jews, Governor Stuyvesant wrote to the company's directors in Amsterdam in October, 1655 that "Giving them liberty we cannot refuse the Lutherans and the Papists."

What was true of New Amsterdam was also true of the other colonies as well as Old World prejudices transplanted to America. These included strong anti-Jewish feelings in Europe in the 17th and 18th centuries. In addition most of the colonies were organized by particular groups or sects for themselves and their own to the exclusion of others. In this immigrant New Amsterdam society the Jews as being different were resented and rejected as intruders. The fact that they were needed made them grudgingly accepted. Land was plentiful, people were not. Individuals with skills and organizational ability were a welcome commodity for the colony. The Jews of colonial America were merchants whose skills and enterprise were needed.[48] There were skilled craftsmen working in wood and metal, tailors, shoemakers and saddlers, bakers butchers. Many were storekeepers and peddlers. There were Jewish fur traders who reached out to the outermost trading posts. It was their place in shipping and ocean commerce that made the Jews a factor in the economic growth of Colonial America. Their ships carried the yield of American fields and forests to Europe and brought back to the colonies the textiles, implements and luxuries of the Old World. The complicated steps involved in disposing of cargoes abroad and obtaining return cargoes were greatly facilitated by their friends and relatives in Amsterdam, London, Lisbon and other European ports. Not all the Jewish merchants in colonial America who traded at home or overseas achieved wealth and distinction. Most of them remained in the low income brackets and they were all exposed to the risks and perils which the entrepreneur faced in those days. There was however in New York Lewis Moses Gomez, a refugee from Spain and later from France, and his six sons. There was Moses Levy whose son was a leading fur trader and at one time the employer of John Jacob Astor. There was Jacob Franks, son-in-law of Moses Levy who became one of the wealthiest men.[49]

The Jew's very existence was dependent on his self-reliance, initiative, daring and perspicacity, qualities which peculiarly fitted him in the colonial scene. Friedman writes that "in a way the role of the Jew has been that of pioneering. By forces of economic and social discrimination and persecution, he has been restricted to participate in a limited number of occupations. His aptitudes, character and achievements are the products therefore of regional historical forces and circumstances."[50]

Another factor for their acceptance was the fact too that life in the New Amsterdam colony was uncertain, precarious—neighbor depended upon neighbor. It led to independence and lastly to acceptance. The expanding frontier community was a challenge for the Jewish community. Small in number, they struggled to establish themselves economically, to be accepted socially and to secure political rights.

During the Dutch period, the Jews were required by law to live in a separate section of the city. There is some evidence to indicate this earliest Jewish neighborhood was on Whitehall Street, near the tip of Manhattan Island. When the British took the city in 1664, the Dutch law lost its force. After that, the Jews moved closer to one another mainly because of their desire to be near their synagogue and other members of their faith. Throughout the colonial period, the section in which the Jews lived was near the Mill Street Synagogue.[51]

Religious Intolerance

What did the New Amsterdamers think of the Jews? The typical American of the seventeenth and eighteenth centuries, a nominal Protestant, considered the Jews objectionable. The very word Jew evoked something negative in the minds of many, if not most of their neighbors.[52] The earliest American colonists were Europeans who had brought with them the bigotries of Europe. What the New Amsterdamer construed as their religious infidelity appeared offensive to them. The Jews were different; that sufficed to render them suspect. At the same time, the Dutch Reformed Minister in New Amsterdam could speak contemptuously of Catholics, Mennonites, Lutherans, Puritans and Atheists, all of whom he lumped and damned together.

The early Christian settler was interested almost solely in his own limited confessional group. He thought it a mistake to show too much courtesy to Jews, for if Jews were encouraged, dissenting Christians would also have to be tolerated. Marcus calls attention to the fact that so many dissenters—and everyone was a dissenter somewhere—made their way to the American colonies, which meant that religious prejudice was never to be focused on the Jew alone, so that although some laws redolent of European Judeophobia were transplanted here, no legislation was ever deliberately and maliciously enacted here to oppress him. New Amsterdam, however, in the mid 1650s was an exception to the last statement. For there, Marcus maintains, as nowhere else in Protestant North America, the attempt was made to transplant and maintain medieval and anti-Jewish law.[53]

Most Christians of the seventeenth and eighteenth centuries were convinced that the baptismal waters would wash away any evil in the souls of the Jews. By contrast with anti semitism, the Judeophobia to which the medieval and early modern Christian responded was largely dissipated when the Jew embraced Christianity. The Christian was eager to bring the Jew into the Christian fold. Marcus calls attention to the fact that it was not a desire to destroy the Jew which prompted both church and state to legislate against the Jew from the fourth century on; rather, that it was a desire to convert him. That desire never waned. As a consequence, Jews were always and everywhere exposed to social prejudice.[54]

Here in the colonies, the Christians believed that America was their country, a Christian country, and they could never envisage America as a homeland for Jews as well as Christians. It was seen during the early American period as a haven for all Christian sects—Catholics excepted. From Marcus's point of view, many of the objections and prejudices voiced against the Jew in America were nothing more than rationalizations of economic envy.[55] He supports this position by referring to Governor Stuyvesant's argument that "to give liberty to the Jews will be very detrimental in New Amsterdam because the Christians will not be able at the same time to do business." When was a Jew not a Jew? When he was not one's competitor, and money was to be made through him. James Beekman might sneer at Jews as a group but he was only too happy to do business respectfully with Moses Franks of London or a Hayman Levy of New York.[56]

The first Jews who came to New Amsterdam, though they might have expected the extensive liberties they had enjoyed in Recife or would have received in Holland herself, found themselves denied religious and economic freedom. As an example, the treatment the merchant David Ferera suffered in New Amsterdam reflects the antagonism a Jew risked there. Found guilty of having insulted a bailiff in a case which involved no moral turpitude, Ferera was arrested and held without bail. The sheriff demanded he be fined, publicly flogged, and banished from the colony. The sentence first pronounced against him was an order to pay the very substantial sum of 800 guilders plus costs. Although the amount was reduced, after reconsideration, Ferera still had to pay a fine of about 170 guilders. Marcus writes that the sheriff's brutal recommendations and the heavy fine Ferera was at length required to pay were motivated by a vindictive anti-Jewish prejudice.[57]

Anti-Jewish incidents were not restricted to the Dutch. They were also known under English rule, too. When Balthazar D'Haert of New York was charged in 1668 with cheating the Jewish merchant Rabba Couty, in a transaction involving flour found to be unusable, D'Haert thought to exculpate himself on the ground that the flour had been only "for a devilish Jew." Governor Stuyvesant was perhaps America's closest approach to the dyed-in-the-wool Jewhater, and even he finally gave up trying to oust the Jews from New Amsterdam.[58]

How did the early Jewish frontiersman earn a livelihood? There was definite hostility to the entry of Jewish competition both in the colony and in foreign trade; the argument was the family connection they enjoyed gave them an advantage over the other traders.

Handicapped by Dutch restrictions, some of the early Jewish

settlers traded with the Indians or were butchers. Asser Levy built an abattoir with a Christian partner in the 1660s on what is today Wall Street, and he also traded in furs. Benjamin Frank was a jeweler, Isaac Moses was a shipowner. Some engaged in domestic trade, some exported wheat. There were others who handled brandy, butter, tobacco. Many were involved in the fur trade. Beaver pelts figured so prominently in the economy that they actually became a legal media for exchange. When Stuyvesant and his Council tried to restrict the Jews from fur trading, the latter under their own group wrote a formal protest to the Dutch West Indies Company in Amsterdam, who were very much interested in trade, and consequently the Jews won the right to enter the fur trade.[59] Lady Katie Magnus writes that it is interesting to note how soon they came to hold land in New York despite Stuyvesant's malice, how in the same city certain retail trades fell entirely into their hands. How Hayman Levy, the fur-trader, was loved by the Indians, how Jacob Rodrigues Rivera died and left a tidy sum in the amount of $120,000, and how Aaron Lopez sent out to the world's harbors twenty-seven vessels.[60]

Rejection: Acceptance

Marcus writes that rejection does not tell the whole story; there was acceptance too, and the bald fact is that the Jews enjoyed a measure of acceptance in carrying on business, conducting their religious services, and in the New Amsterdam colony winning limited political and economic rights with the help of their co-religionists in Holland. He began to see that America reserved her most thorough-going hostility, not for the Jew, but for the Catholic. He knew too that while Europe always harbored a sizeable number of Christians who nursed a pathologically venomous hatred for Jews, such men were at the most exceedingly rare in colonial America, with Stuyvesant the closest to the dyed-in-the-wool Jew hater, and even he finally gave up on ousting the Jews from the colony.[61]

In the New Amsterdam colony, the Jew had to associate with his Gentile neighbors, all of whom he knew and to many of whom he had to, as shopkeeper, extend credit. That the Gentile tended to like and trust the Jewish shopkeeper is manifest in the fact of his patronage. Villagers who met in the streets several times a day learned to know each other well. The townspeople who gossiped over back fences developed an understanding of one another. Trade was often at the root of Jewish-Christian friendships. However, this should not be emphasized to the exclusion of other factors. Christians sought out Jews to discuss theology and to learn Hebrew; relationships sprung up often out of a need for companionship or the fact that they had the same Old World background. They were also drawn together by common experiences. Relations between Jews and Gentiles are reflected in the legal documents. Even during the 1600s, Asser Levy had not been exceptional in being called on to witness wills and to serve as trustee for various estates. Jews and Christians often witnessed one another's wills. Jews were not uncommonly appointed administrators of Christian estates.[62]

Jewish Rights in Colonial Times

Religious liberty, political freedom and economic freedom were each in turn the magnetic attraction which drew the Jews to America. In colonial days it was religious intolerance which drove Jewish emigration to America when a universal Catholic Church, by its Inquisition, struggled to maintain a totalitarian control over religious thinking.[63]

The interaction of Jewish forces with the early American scene as manifested in the expanding rights of the Jewish minority and in the growing recognition that Jews were people who were aspiring to full civic equality is a theme with tremendous meaning in both

Jewish history and in the development of democratic principles as we in this country understand them.[64]

For the 23 unwanted refugees who arrived in New Amsterdam in 1654, it was a constant fight for survival. First, they had to pit themselves as a group with their co-religionists in Amsterdam against the bigotry of Governor Stuyvesant and his Council of Nine for the right to remain in the colony. Then it was an uphill struggle to pray together in public, to secure ground for a cemetery, to build a synagogue. Finally it was a struggle with much persistence and persuasion to secure for themselves citizen rights as well as economic rights. Marcus writes the small Jewish community were ready always to do battle. They stood up to Stuyvesant for the right to stand guard and to eliminate the discriminating military tax, directed against Jews, not only because some were too poor to pay the tax but because it was bound up with the burgher license which in turn was tied up with the privilege of denization. They could not forego their right to do business, which was tied up with citizenship. By June 14, 1654 Jews were permitted to trade. By 1657 they had fought for and secured the right to full citizenship, shared in the defense of the city, and owned property. They had also secured written permission to practice their religion "in all quietness within their home." Though forbidden to build a synagogue, they were granted permission to organize a congregation which they called Shearith Israel. The New Amsterdam colony had regulations prohibiting any public religious gathering of any other religion except by the Dutch Reformed Church, which alone was permitted to erect religious buildings. English dissenters, Quakers as well as Dutch Lutherans, were harshly discriminated against. There was constant strife between Stuyvesant, a tyrant who cared little for the interests of the citizenry, and his Council of Nine men who were named to be his advisers as representative of the people. One of their duties was to promote the preservation of the pure Reformed Religion. Church and State thus in New Amsterdam were yoked together.[65]

The first victory over Peter Stuyvesant's bigotry was more than an entering wedge for achieving further civil rights. It paved the way for other religious sects to assert themselves and win their rights.

In 1655, Stuyvesant ordered the Jews exempt from military and guard duty. They were subject to a military tax for every male between 16 and 65 of 65 stivers a month. Asser Levy and Jacob Barsimon challenged the ruling. Levy was American Jewry's first leader. His real name was Asser Levy van Swellam, an Ashkenazi Jew, a native of Amsterdam who had lived in Brazil until forced to flee. After arriving in New Amsterdam, he dropped his Dutch name, retaining only Asser Levy as his name. Together in 1655 they objected to the discriminating military tax, and petitioned for the right to stand guard in defense of the town. The court of Burgomaster not only rejected their pleas but told them to leave the colony. When Levy stood guard in defiance of the local authorities, he became the first Jewish soldier in America. By the Spring of 1657 Levy was serving in the guard like any ordinary citizen.[66]

A year and a half later he presented another petition, to say that inasmuch as he had been a burgher in Amsterdam, keeping watch and ward like other New Amsterdam citizens, he requested full burgher status. Again the court turned his request down, but finally ruled in his favor. Thus Asser Levy won not only for himself but for his fellow Jews the right to citizenship. That same year Jews won the right to share in the defense of the city, the right to trade anywhere in New Netherlands and the right to own property. Going back a little, in a letter dated November 29, 1655 signed by Abraham de Lucena, Salvador Dandrada and Jacob Cohen, together they had petitioned for the right to trade with the Indians on the Delaware and Hudson. Their request was at first also turned down by Stuyvesant, but in 1657 after repeated effort and help from abroad the Jews were given the right to trade anywhere in New Netherlands. It was Salvador Dandrada who had attempted to buy a home which was at first denied him whereupon the Jewish community as a group made a direct petition to Stuyvesant. This too was turned down. With the help once again from the Jews in Holland, they finally secured the right to own real estate. Thus these social and economic rights wrung from Stuyvesant permitted the Jews a period of some security. It was Asser Levy until his death in 1680 who played a leading role in the fight for political and economic rights in the New Amsterdam colony. At first he was a butcher and he built an abattoir. Later he bought furs from the Indians and became a fur trader. He also owned considerable property in "Breucklyn" and Long Island.[67]

The Burgher Rights Law covered two classes of citizenry in New Amsterdam: a) exclusive great burgher right with a high fee that suggested an attempt to found a provincial aristocracy and b) the small burgher right which became a requirement for anyone running a business, the cost of which was 20 guilders.

Actually, therefore, Asser Levy's claim to the small burgher right was a test case.[68] He won; it was a victory not only for himself, it was a victory for the rest of the Jews in the New Amsterdam colony and strengthened the group ties of other religious sects in the colony as well. Their successes obtained benefits not only for themselves but also opened the door for other disenfranchised groups.[69]

Crime for a Jew To Sell at Retail

It was a crime for a Jew to sell at retail. Jews were barred from engaging in the retail trade. On March 1, 1655 Abraham de Lucena was summoned to court on two charges: 1) keeping the store open on Sunday and 2) selling at retail. It was a violation of the existing law for any citizen to do business on Sunday, but to sell at retail was a normally perfectly legal transaction. It was a crime, however, only for Jews! In practice, though, this was not too strictly adhered to, for a heavy fine was not imposed on de Lucena.

In April 1657 Jacob Cohen Henriques asked permission to bake and sell bread as other bakers did. He received permission to conduct his business as a "wholesale" venture. The ban against participation in the retail trade was also influenced by the fact that Jews had been active in the overseas trade with their numerous family connections abroad and in the West Indies. It is impossible, Goodman writes, to learn just how long Jews were forbidden to sell at retail. There is no record of the withdrawal of the ban. What is evident is that within 40 years Jews were conducting shops without hindrance. There was, for example, Solomon Myers who was made a freeman of the city of New York in 1724. The old list tells us he was a shopkeeper. Evidently, the Jews in that trade enjoyed a legitimate status at the time. Peter Kalm, the Finnish university professor who visited New York in 1748, remarked that the Jews were allowed to keep shops in town.[70]

Another field closed to Jews by the Dutch was handicrafts. The eighteenth century saw the entry of a number of Jews into skilled trades. For example, in 1716 Abraham Pereira, the tallow chandler, was admitted to the rolls, to be followed by a baker, tailor, and brazier, all invested with the rights and privileges of freeman.[71]

Many of the Jewish disabilities were based on precedents in Amsterdam which the directors themselves had invoked. For example, in the Dutch metropolis, Jews were not permitted to conduct retail business or work at handicrafts. Goodman writes: "In the campaign for emancipation which was now opening on American soil, the energetic attachment of the Jews in regard to freedom to participate in trades, was patterned on the tradition of Amsterdam."[72]

The economic and political "charter" in the colony was the letter of the West India Company ordering Stuyvesant to allow the Jews to travel to the colony and to trade in it. It was a charter of limited rights such as the denial of the right to keep a shop and to sell at retail which stemmed from the traditional guild restraints imposed on Jewry in Europe. Marcus calls attention, therefore, to the fact that the Jews of New Amsterdam were second-class burghers, citizens with circumscribed economic liberties. He also notes that though they were called burghers and were formally granted burgher rights by the Dutch, they are not found in the late 1650's in the official list of the "freemen" of the town.[73]

The political and economic rights won from the Dutch were maintained when the English took over the colony in 1664 and renamed it New York. The Jews were expected to conform to the old world guild restrictions of not entering a retail trade or practicing a craft. Marcus writes: "Onerous as these disabilities seem now, they in reality were not very formidable. In reality, the Jews practiced their crafts if they possessed them, and no one 'in this raw young country stopped them' for craftsmen were in great demand."[74]

The position of the Dutch and English colonial Jewry therefore followed a pattern of compromise. On the one hand, the guild, craft, restrictions remained. On the other hand, these Jews appeared on the colonial scene at a period of developing mercantilism and of developing the colonies to export to continental Europe the wealth this country had in terms of tobacco, fish, furs, wheat, rice and other farm products which called for hands to draw it forth. The trading companies, therefore, tolerated and encouraged the Jews in commerce and industry.[75] Jews were prepared to grasp the opportunity. They directed their attention not primarily at the repeal of limiting laws but at the functional exercise of rights officially denied them.[76]

Equal Justice and a Fair Trial

Did the Jews as a minority enjoy fair and objective handling in the court? Prejudice was definitely a factor to be reckoned with in the courts of justice. An example of mishandling in the court was David de Ferera in New Amsterdam. The Dutch authorities were "thin skinned" and responded violently to criticism and seeming discourtesy. There was a dispute over a contract and in connection therewith, the court of burgomasters and schepens in 1656 ordered de Ferera to deliver some goods to a creditor of one of his judgment debtors. De Ferera first left them with the creditor, then carted them away. He was fined 800 guilders, which was a huge sum, in addition to costs. In default, he was kept in jail for almost a month and also denied bail. On appeal to the Director General, de Ferera was released on payment of a much more moderate fine fixed by arbitration.

It is pertinent to refer to a classic speech made by Edmund Burke wherein he brings up the close connection which existed in America between dissent and liberty. This has definite bearing on the Dutch colony of New Amsterdam where bigotry and religious inequality and persecution presided. Burke brings up the point that had there been no dissenters, no minority groups, the issue of civil liberties might seldom have been raised.[77] In the Colonial Period each dissenting sect, each minority, religious or ethnic acted as a catalyst to accelerate demands for equal rights.

Small in numbers, lacking figures of great intellectual attainment or political stature, the Jews in the colonial period made their most significant impact in the field of civil liberties. In the colonies, the first right for which the Jews fought was that of settlement as aliens and non-Christians. The fact that the Jews were fighting the battle of other minority groups as well is clear from Stuyvesant's rejoinder to the company. "Giving the Jews liberty, we cannot refuse the Lutherans and Papists." The Directors pointed out that what was granted to the Jews was civil liberties, not the right publicly to exercise their religion.[78]

There is abundant evidence to show that where the Jews gained the equal protection of the laws other minorities were likely to profit thereby and that the struggle of Presbyterian minorities or French Huguenot minorities or German Pietist Minorities or Catholic minorities was inseparably related to the security of the

Jewish community. In fact, had there been no minority groups in this country, colonial and early America would have been quite differently structured and doubtless less vital and democratic than they were in fact. At least forty per cent of the population of the American colonies was of non-English stock, and the followers of the Church of England established in a number of the colonies were in fact a numerical minority. Accordingly, toleration and equal rights were the keys to effective operation of government. Without them discord and civil strife would have stifled opportunity, discouraged immigration, and caused a breakdown of law enforcement.[79]

SUMMARY:

Jews have been in the Western Hemisphere from its first contact with Europeans. From the first there was occupational diversity and geographic scattering. The first organized Jewish community in the colonies was established in New Amsterdam. They were the 23 Jews from Recife, Brazil who came here in family units. The family has always been the vehicle for the transmitting of Jewish folkways and mores. Their social structure was embodied in the "synagogue" which both controlled and guided their lifestyle. From the very first there was insistence on civil rights and religious equality. The endured travail and tenacity demonstrated by this group in the day to day struggle to overcome the anti-Jewish medieval law which Stuyvesant had transplanted to New Amsterdam is equally balanced by the tightly knit social fabric of this community, between individual and group first in the colony and then reinforced by their co-religionists in Holland. It should also not be overlooked that some of the Directors and influential members of the trading company were Jews and it was in their best interests to maintain Holland as the leader in international trade at the time, to which the Jews contributed in full measure with their skills and experience. The Jews in New Amsterdam did fight for the right of settlement as aliens and non-Christians, and in their uphill struggle for civil rights and religious freedom were also fighting the battle of other minority groups. Though it was limited burgherhood with the Dutch, under the English towards the middle of the eighteenth century, with the Naturalization Law they were to enjoy a greater freedom. In addition, though the early Jews were resented at first by their Christian neighbors and looked upon with suspicion, the harsh frontier life fraught with its dangers drew them a little closer together, particularly in the day to day social interaction where Jews were shopkeepers, fur traders, merchants. Curiosity developed too with time to find out more about the Hebrew language and about the Jews and their religion. There was attendance of both Christian and Jews at ground-breaking ceremonies for church and synagogue. With time, therefore, it can be said that while Jews were tolerated in the colony, it even went beyond that with intermarriage. Asser Levy's business partner was a Christian. Jews and Christians were witnesses for each other in drawing up wills. It can be said that the first Jewish organized community made an impact on the colony and also made a significant contribution in the areas of civil rights and freedom of religion for themselves and other groups.

The experiences that the early American Jews had accumulated in the course of wanderings and adaptations were of great help to them in their struggle to find a place in the colonial economy. The fortunate circumstances that the colony was ready to receive what the Jews had to offer in the way of their skills and services are also responsible for their solid achievements here. The Sephardic Jews brought with them a mercantilist background which they put to good use in domestic business and international trade. This was of considerable value to the young colonies which needed an independent economy at home and outlets of their own abroad. Frederick J. Turner characterized the frontier as the point where savagery and civilization met.[80] The Jew of the seventeenth century of the New Amsterdam, later renamed New York colony, was very much a part of this scene. Here on the frontier where a premium was placed upon individual strength, courage, inventiveness and initiative, a new individualism was born[81] and the Jew of the seventeenth century characterizes this type, the individual who stood up and dared to challenge the established authority with all its anti-Jewish prejudice, in the search for both freedom of opportunity and freedom of worship. The first Jewish community originating from Recife in no small measure has made its indelible impact on the warp and woof of the American social and political fabric and more recent research has laid to rest the past Anglocentric bias. What has emerged has been the factual acknowledgment that the early Jewish pioneers by their steadfast struggle and facing up to the bigotry and anti-semitism of Stuyvesant won battle after battle in their fight for political and economic freedom, of a limited nature, not only for their own community since their successes also helped ethnic groups other than the established Dutch Reformed Church. Thus it can be said in re-examining early American life in the New Amsterdam colony that the first Jewish settlement made a significant contribution in laying the ground for political pluralism in the developing American scene.

Naturalization

The Naturalization Laws passed by the British Parliament on June 1, 1740 brought to the Jews of New York their first taste of freedom and equality. Under the new act, you had to be a resident of one of the American colonies for seven continuous years, allowing only two months' absence, and then you had to take an Oath of Abjuration.[82]

S. Meyer Cohen, a butcher was the first Jew to become a citizen in 1740 when the Naturalization Law was passed.[83]

Some of the other early citizens were:[84]

David Gomez
Mardy Gomez
Don Gomez
Jacob ferro Jur
Sam Levy
Isaac Levy

Solomon Neve
David Hays
Abram Rio de Rivera
Daniel Rodrigues Venera
Solomon Meyer
Jo Simson

GLOSSARY

1. abattoir—slaughterhouse built by the Jews to take care of their need.
2. burgher rights—rights of citizenship which included also the requirements for running a business, the cost of which was 20 guilders.
3. cemetery—served as the permanent geographic nuclear unit of community organization.
4. denization—temporary right to do business in the colony.
5. esnoga—Portuguese word for synagogue—this is what the Jews in Recife called their house of worship.
6. gemilat hasadim—Financial help given to a family by the synagogue to help them get started towards independence.
7. hakhnassat orhim—Temporary shelter given to needy arrivals by the synagogue.
8. hazzan—In early colonial days, there was no rabbi in the New Amsterdam colony; the hazzan read the service, for which he was paid £50 a year, given 6 cords firewood, enough matzoh for family.
9. hooflparticipanten—chief shareholders in the Dutch East and Dutch West Indies Company.

10. home of life—burial grounds, so called by the Jews in New Amsterdam.
11. junta—board of officers of the synagogue.
12. kahal—social structure of the Jews in Europe where they had certain restrictions but also still had certain rights of self-government.
13. minder participanten—minor shareholders in the Dutch West Indies Company.
14. minyan—Under the laws of Judaism, 10 adults, male Jews of any locality, coming together in one place are necessary for public worship, which can be in a field, under a tree or in a home.
15. mitzvot—Early Jews included the reading of blessings as another form of raising money for synagogue maintenance.
16. parnas—president of the synagogue who collected and kept the synagogue records, maintained the discipline, imposed fines, awarded honors.
17. synagogue—social structure of the Jewish community. Embraced the social, religious, political and educational as well as the authority of the community. Giving financial aid and any other was also considered a vital part of its function. In New Amsterdam, it was "the community" as against it being only one agency as in Europe. It represented the first Jewish institutional organization which was a "collective concern."
18. shammas—He assisted the hazzan. His salary was £16 a year, plus wood and matzoh. He kept the synagogue clean and saw that candles were always on hand.

BIBLIOGRAPHY

De Sola Pool, David. *Portraits Etched in Stone*. New York: Columbia University Press, 1952.

Frank, Isaac: "The Changing American Jewish Community," *American Jewry*. New York: The Reconstructionist Press, 1955.

Friedman, Lee M. *Jewish Pioneers and Patriots*. Philadelphia: The Jewish Publication Society of America, 1942.

Glazer, Nathan. *American Judaism*. Second Edition Revised. Chicago: The University of Chicago Press, 1972.

Grinstein, Hyman B. *The Rise of the Jewish Community of New York 1654-1860*. Philadelphia: The Jewish Publication Society of America, 1945.

Goodman, Abram Vossen. *American Overture: Jewish Rights in Colonial Time*. Philadelphia: The Jewish Publication Society of America, 1947.

Handlin, Oscar. *Adventure in Freedom*. New York: McGraw-Hill Book Company, 1954.

Karp, Abraham J. Editor. *The Jewish Experience in America: I— The Colonial Period*. American Jewish Historical Society, Waltham, Mass. New York: Ktav Publishing House, Inc., 1969.

Kohn, Eugene, Editor. "The Tercentenary and After," *American Jewry*. New York: The Reconstructionist Press, 1955.

Lebesman, Anita Libman. "The American Jewish Chronicle," *The Jews, Their History, Culture, and Religion*, edit. by Louis Finkelstein. New York: Harper & Bros., 1949, Volume I.

Learsi, Rufus. *The Jews in America*. Cleveland: World Publishing Company, 1954.

Magnus, Katie (Lady). *Outlines of Jewish History*. Philadelphia: The Jewish Publication Society of America, 1929.

Marcus, Jacob Rader. *Early American Jewry; 1649-1794*. Philadelphia: The Jewish Publication Society of America, 1951.

—— *The Colonial American Jew 1492-1776*. Detroit: The University Press, 1970. Volume III.

Mulder, Arnold. *Americans From Holland*. New York: J. P. Lippincott & Co., 1947.

Old Whalers Festival Journal, Sag Harbor, New York, 1967.

Oppenheim, Samuel. *The Early History of the Jews in New York 1654-1664*. New York: The American Historical Society, 1909.

Postal, Bernard & Koppman, Lionel. *Jewish Landmarks in New York*. New York: Hill and Wang, Inc., 1964.

Roth, Cecil. *A History of the Marranos*. New York: Meridian Books, Inc., 1959, Philadelphia: The Jewish Publication Society of America, 1932.

Sachar, Abram Leon. *A History of The Jews*, 4th Edition. New York: Alfred A. Knopf, 1960.

Savelle, Max. *Seeds of Liberty: The Genesis of the American Mind*. Seattle: University of Washington Press, 1948.

Schappes, Morris U. Editor. *A Documentary History of the Jews in the United States 1654-1875*. Third Edition. New York: Schocken Books, 1970.

St. John, Robert. *Jews, Justice and Judaism*. Garden City, New York: Doubleday & Company, Inc., 1969.

FOOTNOTES

[1] Jacob Rader Marcus, *Early American Jewry*, Philadelphia: The Jewish Publication Society of America, 1951, xii, xv.

[2] Marcus, *Ibid.*, 15, 17.

[3] Nathan Glazer, *American Judaism*, Chicago: University of Chicago Press, 1972, Second Edition, 12. 13.

[4] David De Sola Pool, *Portrait Etched in Stone*, New York: Columbia University Press, 1952, 4. 5. Abraham J. Karp, editor, *The Jew in America: The Colonial Period*, New York: Ktav Publishing Co., Inc., 1969, preface XII, XIII.

[5] Abram Leon Sachar, *A History of the Jews*, New York: Alfred A. Knopf, 1960, 230.

[6] Samuel Oppenheim, "The Early History of the Jews in New York 1654-1664," *The Jews in America*, edited by Abraham Karp, 14, 16.

[7] Cecil Roth, *A History of the Marranos*, New York: Meridian Books Inc., 1959, and the Jewish Publication Society of America, 1959, Philadelphia, 19, 20.

[8] Rufus Learsi, *The Jews in America*, Cleveland: World Publishing Co., 1954, 16.

[9] Anita Libman Leveson, "The American Chronicle," *The Jew, Their History, Culture & Religion*, edited by Louis Finkelstein, New York: Harper & Bros., 1949, Vol. I, 316-317.

[10] Cecil Roth, 285-289. De Sola Pool, 6.

[11] Marcus, 22.

[12]Arnold Wiznitzer, "The Exodus from Brazil and Arrival in New Amsterdam of the Jewish Pilgrim Fathers, 1654," *The Jew in America: The Colonial Period*, 26.
[13]*Ibid.*, 31.
[14]Reprinted from the 1967 Old Whalers Festival Journal, Sag Harbor, N.Y.
[15]Robert St. John, *Jews, Justice and Judaism*, Garden City, N.Y.: Doubleday & Co., Inc., 1969, 11.
[16]Wiznitzer, 31.
[17]Leveson, 317.
[18]Oscar Handlin, *Adventures in Freedom*, New York: McGraw & Hill Book Co., 3.
[19]Leon Hubner, "A Noted Jewish Burgher of New Amsterdam," *The Jew in America: The Colonial Period*, 51.
[20]Abram Voss Goodman, *American Overture: Jewish Rights in Colonial Times*, Philadelphia: The Jewish Publication Society of America, 1947, 85.
[21]Samuel Oppenheim, "More About Jacob Barsiman, The First Jewish Settler in New York," The Jews in America: The Colonial Period, Vol. I, 37, 38.
[22]Oppenheim, 40, 47.
[23]*Ibid.*
[24]Leon Huhner, 51-52. See also documents relating to Colonial History volume XIV, 315.
[25]Bernard Postal & Lionel Koppman, *Jewish Landmarks in New York*, New York: Hill and Wang, Inc., 1964, 11.
[26]Hyman B. Grinstein, *The Rise of the Jewish Community of New York 1654-1860*, Philadelphia: The Jewish Publication Society of America, 1945, 30.
[27]Glazer, 18.
[28]Rufus Learsi, 28.
[29]Nathan Glazer, 20.
[30]De Sola Pool, 17.
[31]*Ibid.*
[32]Learsi, 38.

[33] Robert St. John, 37-38.
[34] Isaac Franck, "The Changing American Jewish Community," *American Jewry*, New York: The Reconstructionist Press, 1955, 18, 19, 20, 27.
[35] Franck, 20.
[36] Leveson, 360-361. Samuel Dinin, "American Influences on Jewish Education," *American Jewry*, 94-95.
[37] Grinstein, 316.
[38] Robert St. John, 28.
[39] *Ibid.*, 29.
[40] *Ibid.*, 30.
[41] *Ibid.*, 31. Also Bernard Postal & Lionel Koppman, 91.
[42] Grinstein, Appendix III, 479.
[43] *Ibid.*, Appendix I, 469.
[44] *Ibid.* Also Miller, *New York Considered and Improved*, p. 54.
[45] *Ibid.*, Appendix V, 485.
[46] *Ibid.*
[47] Jacob Rader Marcus, *The Colonial American Jew 1492-1776*, Detroit: The University Press, 1970, Volume III, 1115.
[48] Abraham J. Karp, Editor, *The Jewish Experience in America*, preface XII-XIV.
[49] Learsi, 35.
[50] Lee M. Friedman, *Jewish Pioneers and Patriots*, Philadelphia, Jewish Publication Society of America, 1942, 5.
[51] Grinstein, 30, 31.
[52] Marcus, 1123.
[53] Marcus, 1123. See also Morris U. Schappes, Ed. *A Documentary History of the Jews in the U.S. 1654-1875*, New York: Schocken Books, 1971, Preface VI, VII. Also Arnold Mulder, *Americans From Holland*, New York: Lippincott & Co., 1947, 40.
[54] *Ibid.*, 1115.
[55] *Ibid.*, 1122.
[56] *Ibid.*
[57] *Ibid.*, 1135.
[58] *Ibid.*

[59] Abram Voss Goodman, 90. Postal & Koppman, 59.
[60] Lady Katie Magnus, *Outlines of Jewish History*, Philadelphia: The Jewish Publication Society of America, 1945, 346.
[61] Marcus, 1135.
[62] Marcus, 1157.
[63] Lee Friedman, 6.
[64] Abram Vossen Goodman, Preface VII.
[65] Voss Goodman, 69, 70. Robert St. John, 11.
[66] Postman & Koppman, 51. Marcus, 30.
[67] Robert St. John, 13.
[68] Abram Voss Goodman, 9, 95, 99.
[69] Marcus, 32.
[70] Goodman, 106.
[71] Goodman, 116.
[72] *Ibid.*, 74, 85, 86.
[73] Marcus, 40.
[74] Marcus, 34.
[75] Handlin, 9.
[76] Marcus, 40.
[77] Richard B. Morris, "Civil Liberties and the Jewish Tradition in Early America," *The Jews in America*, 419.
[78] Morris, 409-410.
[79] Morris, 423.
[80] C. Bezalel Sherman, "Jewish Economic Adjustment," *American Jewry*, 46, 47.
[81] Max Savelle, *Seeds of Liberty*, Seattle: University of Washington Press, 1948, 243.
[82] Menasseh Vaxer, *Naturalization Roll of New York 1740-1759*, American Jewish Historical Society #37, 1947, 369, 370.
[83] Postal and Koppman, 53.
[84] Vaxer, 373.

A Comparison of Two Societies: Israel and the People's Republic of China

The People's Republic of China, a revolutionary totalitarian society dedicated to class struggle, and the State of Israel, a parliamentary democracy, are twentieth century phenomena, and as such invite interest for comparison and analysis.

Ideologically opposite, they are 1) highly motivated societies and 2) group and community oriented. For both countries the goals of education are pragmatic and are geared to fit in with the needs and development of the total society. Similarly, the concept of national identity and social cohesion lies in the people themselves. In China this cohesion has been furthered by the Maoist monopoly of print and advertising, the Party committees at all levels and the People's Liberation Army and security system. Behind this lies the well-integrated self concepts that put the moral concerns for one's neighbors and the community above the self, the Maoist philosophy of the selfless. Equally, the Israelis are a tightly knit nationalistic society, devoted with fervor and tenacity to country and defending her with the same strength and singlemindedness. Both systems have strong national unity and commitment. In the case of Israel, it is furthered by the constant threat to their survival, and for the People's Republic of China it is expressed by deep-rooted resentment against past exploitation from within their country and without.

Critically, there has been increasing recognition of the importance of including the political experiences of Communist China in comparative studies in the formulation of valid generalizations about political phenomena. Communist China is not only one of the most significant examples of totalitarian rule but also one of the most significant experiments in modernization.[1]

The China Experience

Mao Tse-tung has been both a symbol and an inspiration. His sayings can be found everywhere—big red or black characters on white village walls, or white on a red background in city parks and public buildings. Visitors to China today see China not only creating a new technology and a new class structure but under Mao's teachings a far-reaching moral crusade to change the Chinese personality in the direction of self-sacrifice and serving others.[2] Formerly, early training under Confucian gentry elite included putting family duties first, now the new cadre-managers are imbued with a secular faith in Mao's teachings and service to the people as a whole. This is the selfless cooperation and collective effort which is changing the Chinese life tremendously. The quality of China's government under Mao has rested on the assumption that man is an instructable moral animal, that rational instruction and education can improve his conduct, and that leadership consists in showing him by precept and example the right way to proceed.

The Doctrine Formalized

The most important features of Chinese communism (Mao Tse-tung's thoughts) are found in the following areas: the theory of imperialism, the concept of united front, and the nature and function of military activity. Mao's conception of imperialism is an extension of the Leninist theory—applying that theory to revolutionary circumstances in a colonial, semicolonial and semifeudal country. Throughout his analysis, Lenin's attention was directed to the capitalist countries and to the development of capitalism into its international monopoly stage, imperialism. Accepting Lenin's propositions, Mao analyzed the implication of the Leninist theory not from the point of view of capitalism-imperialism, but from the standpoint of the backward countries, particularly China. Mao reasoned that since China is unevenly developed, and since the power of the enemy is concentrated in the urban, industrialized centers, the revolutionaries would have to retreat to the countryside. There with the help of the local population, they would consolidate and strengthen their position, surround the cities and strangle the enemy. The Chinese countryside offered for Mao the indispensable, vital positions of the Chinese revolution because revolutionary villages can encircle the cities, but revolutionary cities cannot detach themselves from the villages. It was only after the revolutionary regime was strong enough that a shift to the urban center could be made. This shift did occur, when on February 8th, 1949 Mao announced the formula followed in the past 20 years, "first the rural areas, then the cities" will be reversed and changed to the formula, "first the cities, then the rural areas."[3]

Infrastructure

The 11th Congress elected a 26 member Politburo, with the new leadership leaning towards a more pragmatic position in its goals. China is presently run by a triumvirate, consisting of Chairman Hua Kuo-feng, Defense Minister Yeh Chien-ying and Deputy Prime Minister Teng Hsiao-ping; Deputy chairman Li Hsien-nien and Wang Tung-hsing are seen as making up the five member Politburo Standing Committee. Many ministerial posts and many seats on the Central Committee also have been open a year or more. This has given rise to thoughts that perhaps power blocs in the country—the party bureaucracy, the army, and various provincial leaders—haven't been able to reach agreement on how much authority will be exercised by each and to agree on replacements to fill the empty jobs.[4] China's present government by exemplary moral men puts a heavy burden on party committees at all levels and cadre (kan-pu) activists who form the network of authority and leadership.

The Chinese Communist regime is a revolutionary, totalitarian movement, operating in a tradition-rooted but changing society. They are attempting not only to create a new policy but also to use political power to modernize China and transform China's social structure and system of values. It has evolved organizational structures and modes of operation from a variety of sources that blend, creating its own unique pattern. This includes the theoretical Leninist model of democratic centralism, the post-Leninist model of Soviet society, the Chinese Communists' own pre-1949 experience in conducting revolutionary struggle, and China's old traditions of authoritarianism, elitism, ideological orthodoxy, and bureaucratic administration.

In a broad sense, they have been able to create a disciplined elite and new structure of Party and government organization which enable a minimal number of Party leaders at the top to enforce their decision-making upon China's enormous population. Policy-making from the center must filter through complex bureaucratic structures of power before they reach and affect the masses. The political apparatus does transmit policy impulses from the center to the grassroots of society in a manner that has never been the case in China before.

Traditionally in China, central power transmitted through a well-established bureaucracy reached the county (hsien) level with some degree of effectiveness, at least during periods when the country was unified under a strong regime, but at subcounty levels "informal government" run by traditional elite groups such as the gentry and by a variety of nongovernmental social institutions tended to dominate the scene. The present Communist regime has basically altered this situation. They have largely destroyed both the old elite groups and most of the traditional social institutions, substituting for them a new Communist Party elite with new Communist-dominated mass organizations, and have extended the formal bureaucratic instruments of Party and government rule down to the village level.[5]

Even more important, the functions of government have been greatly expanded. In pre-Communist China the government generally was content if social order could be maintained and taxes collected. The Communist centrally directed apparatus of political power, however, is designed to change society, not simply to preserve it. The goals include altering the country's basic class structure, reindoctrinating the entire population in a new ideological orthodoxy, changing fundamental patterns of behavior and reorganizing the economy to spur rapid development. The Communist Party considers everything to be of political concern, whether in the field of thought or action. Hence, the society has been politicized to an unprecedented degree. This has involved not only basic changes in the attitudes of leaders as well as the people, but also a great expansion of the organizational apparatus of political power at all levels. New institutions have been built to enable the leaders not only to police the entire society but also to manage the economy in addition to indoctrinating the mass of the population in Marxism-Leninism and the thoughts of Mao Tsetung to achieve the basis for an effective totalitarian political and social system.

Growth of Bureaucratic Structure as Step towards Modernization

Max Weber described modern bureaucracy as a legal rational system of authority characteristic of modern society. Modern bureaucracy is marked by a high degree of structural differentiation and functional specialization. A major concern of a modern bureaucracy is to mobilize organizational resources for efficient task performance and goal achievement based on secular and rational principles. Its system of personnel recruitment, assignment, transfer, and promotion is governed by pre-established, universalistic, impersonal, and achievement-oriented standards.[6]

In an analysis of the expanding Chinese bureaucratic structure, a case study of Wuhan, 1949-65, Yang-Mao Kau posits that since assuming power in 1949, the new Communist leadership in China has given priority to modernization and industrialization among its major national goals. These priorities have helped sustain a rationale by which the state instituted and maintained an extensive system of totalitarian control over China's national life. Replaced by that system, private organizations and enterprises in China were systematically emasculated from 1949 on, and virtually disappeared after the 1956 upsurge of socialist transformation. Since then, the entire nation has come under the control of a unified system of official bureaucracies and their semi-official agents, and the responsibility for achieving national goals has fallen entirely on the state and Party bureaucracies. Thus, before the Great Proletarian Cultural Revolution and its violent assault on the bureaucracies in 1966, it was not an exaggeration to say that the bureaucracies held the key to China's future development.[7]

According to Barnett,[8] the Party has tried in many ways to resist the irresistible growth of complex bureaucratic patterns of social stratification even within the ranks of the Party cadres, for example, by promoting physical labor by cadres, sending personnel to work in rural areas, and taking such drastic steps as abolishing ranks within the army. Apparently what appears to be getting in the way are deep-rooted authoritarian and bureaucratic predispositions, especially the tendency to differentiate people by rank. Consequently, virtually all cadres in Communist China today can be labeled and placed fairly accurately in the hierarchy of power and prestige on the basis of seniority in the Party, salary grade, and job rank. Significantly, while formal salary and job ratings are very important, informal ratings based on length of service in the Party appear to be just as important, and in fact the former tend to be equated with the latter. The growth of these patterns of social stratification according to Barnett has been a major factor contributing to the steady bureaucratization of the regime and the erosion of the elite's revolutionary character.

Stricter Controls on the Bureaucratic Elite

There is stricter discipline and tighter checks on the cadres who make up the bureaucratic elite than on most ordinary people in the society, with the exception of groups treated as public enemies. Detailed dossiers are maintained on all cadres. They are subjected to regular fitness reports which probe their activities and attitudes in great detail. They must participate in regular "study" sessions, where collective group pressures help to enforce conformity and discipline. Any shortcomings or failures on their part expose them to the risk of severe administrative punishment or to the possibility of political attack in "struggle meetings" during periodic "rectification" campaigns. They live in a general atmosphere of restrictive security consciousness, where their lives have been "collectivized" in a fashion which bestows on them the benefits of paternalistic concern for their welfare on the one hand and on the other that of close and continuous surveillance. They are subject to frequent transfers, more often lateral than upward; in recent years often downward, to rural areas, and most of them must participate in some sort of physical work, which the regime promotes to combat bureaucratism.

If they are Party or Young Communist League cadres, they must, in addition, participate actively in "Party Life" or "League Life," which involves regular and frequent group meetings as well as many other demands on their time and energies.[9]

It would appear therefore the cadres in China today have relatively little personal life, are under continual close scrutiny by higher authorities, are also subjected to intense social pressures to submit and conform, and must give continuous evidence of their loyalty and obedience to the regime.

The Mass Line

Communist China relies upon mass campaigns, rather than on more routinized administrative methods, to carry out its major policies and programs. This revolutionary mode of operation was a product of the technique for mass mobilization developed during the struggle for power. The campaign approach to policy implementation, which grows out of commitment to the "mass line," involves the setting up of a few clearly defined immediate aims, concentration of effort on these aims, mobilization and training of large numbers of cadres drawn from many segments of the political system to carry out a campaign, and finally the mass mobilization of the population as a whole to take action to achieve the defined goals. These campaigns rest on the premise that the masses, if they are properly organized and infused with ideological fervor, can be activated to achieve most of the society's fundamental goals. Human will and labor, rather than technical skills, are understood as the key ingredients of social progress. The Communist Party itself rather than other institutions assumes prime responsibilities for directing these campaigns.[10]

Local Government—the Collectivation Movements

The major change in Chinese society can be seen as an increase in the scale and scope of organization. In the countryside the period from 1950 to 1960 began with the destruction of the landlord as a class, though not, in most cases, as individuals, and the more even, though not absolutely equal distribution of land among households. Land reform was followed by a series of collectivation movements, beginning with seasonal mutual aid teams of ten or so households, and ending with the establishment of People's Communes. This meant that some ninety million family farms were replaced by seventy-four thousand communes. A family farm consisted of one household; a commune consists of about sixteen hundred households.

Most communes contain several villages. Today communes are the lowest unit of local government, corresponding in some ways to rural townships in this country. Communes are further subdivided into units called brigades, and brigades are subdivided into teams. Brigades, or production brigades as they are sometimes called, are in fact villages. Production teams consist of perhaps ten to twenty households, all of course from the same village. Land is no longer private property and cannot be bought, rented, nor inherited. Today the basic unit of account, the unit which in effect holds title to land, pays taxes, and sells produce for cash, is, in most cases, the team. The brigade assigns work, such as responsibility for cultivating certain fields or the provision of so many eggs—to teams. Household members work as part of a team. Each person receives a certain number of work points for each day he or she works for the team. At the end of the year the total income of the team, less taxes is divided by the number of work points accumulated. Each person then receives a share, in grain and cash, determined by the number of work points to his credit. Households own their own houses. Each household has, in addition, a private plot on which it grows vegetables for its own consumption and for sale, and which it may use for pigs or chickens. There are several consequences of these changes in land tenure. In the first place, Chinese farmers are now wage earners. Two things determine a family's income. The first is the number of work points its members have accumulated. The second is the total surplus of the team to which it belongs. Brigades with relatively low incomes are urged to rely on their own efforts and to emulate the successful practices of other brigades. Where, however, the income of a household falls below a minimum standard, then the team or brigade will help and make up the difference so that there is adequate food for all the members of the household.[11] In factories and offices wage differentials have been reduced, and wage incentives and bonuses have been replaced by a uniform, standard wage. Units are run by Revolutionary Committees rather than by single managers, and all managers spend some time doing manual labor in the fields or on the shop floor. Workers and farmers are given much more credit for innovations and solutions to problems than specialists or experts. Working diligently in one's organization, applying intelligence in the solution of problems of the organization, are acknowledged as leading to upward social mobility.[12]

Party and State and Society

In a basic sense, "mass mobilization" reflects certain fundamental assumptions about society and the relationships of state and society, more precisely, Party and State and Society, that are inherent in the Communists' "concepts of contradictions and class struggle." To a substantial degree, local cadres, like the Party's top leaders, view society in terms of "class" groupings defined by the Party, also treat people differently on the basis of "class" status, and assume that there can be contradictions between various groups. In many of their mass mobilization activities they consciously attempt to manipulate real or latent tensions between groups and to mobilize certain groups to struggle against others. This manipulative approach to social forces—that is, the management of "contradictions" and the self-conscious utilization of class conflicts—is clearly viewed as necessary to maintain a fairly high level of tension in society (which is in marked contrast to the traditional Chinese view that every effort should be made to harmonize interest and minimize conflicts) and a significant degree of social tension achieved through struggle is believed to be essential for continuing revolution.[13]

The People's Liberation Army

Barbara Tuchman explains the "heavy internal propaganda on armed force and the glory of the gun and the heroic virtues of the People's Liberation Army" in terms of a feeling of encirclement on the part of China prior to 1971. "Reaching down to primary school children who conduct military games and exercises with mock rifles, it is designed to instill military self-confidence and dignify the formerly despised status of the soldier." Tuchman feels the purpose is more defensive than aggressive, that as a Socialist state, the Chinese seem genuinely convinced of their own non-aggressiveness.[14]

While for the present there appear both major and minor changes, with a move to moderation on almost every level, the People's Liberation Army continues to play a significant part in the life of the people. Previously needed to administer many institutions disrupted by the Cultural Revolution, the army is still a major force. P.L.A. men hold about half the seats on the Communist Party Central Committee and the Politburo. In the provinces, over half the chairmen of the governing revolutionary committees and the leaders of the provincial Communist Party hierarchy are army men. They also still hold the chairmanship of the revolutionary committees that run many of the nation's institutions. As an example, Wang Lien-lung, chairman of the revolutionary committee that directs Peking University, is an army man and six other P.L.A. men sit with him on the 39 member committee. There are four army men on the 27-man revolutionary committee running Textile Factory No. 4 in the city of Sian. In 1970 there were two army men on the committee. There are two army men on the 18-man revolutionary committee of Peking Middle School No. 31 as compared to three men last year.[15]

The Cultural Revolution

The Cultural Revolution was not only a power struggle between Mao and Liu Shao-chi, it was also a struggle over basic policy. What Mao feared was that Liu's policies in the Party, the government bureaucracy, the school and the economy were leading in the direction of rule by an urban-based managerial and professional elite, preoccupied with its careers and privileges, out of touch with the farm and factory workers. Mao had seen this happen in Russia and, calling it revisionism, he did not want this to happen in China. He turned the nation's youth loose, the Red Guards from the high schools and colleges to destroy the Party, government and educational bureaucracies. He was looking to rekindle in the youth revolutionary zeal and rebuild the country on more egalitarian lines. After two years of tumult, the People's Liberation Army was called in to restore order and lead the country from chaos.

The Cultural Revolution can be seen as a revolution to establish a propertyless class culture. It has sought to put the process of change into the hands of the people, who were mainly villagers under the necessary guidance of a new leadership, and also eliminate the old evils of the privileged ruling class outlook. The new system has endeavored to do this by making the universities into places where special training could be given village youth to take back and improve production. Both experimental and transitional, the new system points up the problem of how to train farm and city craftsmen in technology and at the same time re-create a modern system as the late twentieth century requires.

The Cultural Revolution was a highly unusual revolution, "an assault by a revolutionary leader against his own post-revolutionary regime," and like other revolutions it is experiencing its Thermidor. Policy has shifted to the right, with restoration of organizational discipline, an accommodative and conciliatory foreign policy, and even signs of intellectual and artistic liberalization. With the purge of Ch'en Po-ta and Lin Piao the coalition which seized power in the Cultural Revolution was aborted. More interestingly, Chou en-lai's diplomatic Grand Design, to offset the Soviet military challenge offered a direct alternative: the possibility of ensuring Chinese security by diplomatic maneuver, by using one superpower to control another. To invite President Nixon to visit China, Chou felt, would be as effective as Lin's plan to construct underground shelters and disperse Chinese industry. One of Crane Brinton's principal conclusions states that although each revolution sees its Thermidor it also leaves a lasting legacy; in the case of China it appears to be the fragmentation of power.[16]

China's Own Industrial Revolution

The agrarian bent of Mao derives from his concern for the common people who live by farming the land. There exists the application of modern technology, developing richer soils and better crops and a new attitude of control over nature. As an example, the Shih-p'ing Brigade in Hsi-yang county, Shansi, learned from its neighbor, the model Tachai Brigade, how to make eroded canyons into fields. The procedure was simply to hand-quarry local stone, transport it to the site and build a network of ten-foot-high stone tunnels two miles long running the length of the canyon floors. It only remained to tear down the canyon walls and fill in the floors to make broad level fields, from which flood waters in the rainy season can drain into the tunnels and harmlessly flow away.

China is intent on avoiding the centralization of industrial growth which would require an enormous transportation network to distribute centrally produced goods to so vast a consuming public. The emphasis, therefore, is partly on local, small-scale production integrated with the collectivized farming communities. The decentralization of industry is seen with the dotting of tall chimneys in almost every rural landscape as well as the big plants in out-of-the way places. Truck traffic is quite marked on rural arteries. Decentralization appears to foster local self-sufficiency, and not only makes for a more balanced rural development, but also has defensive value against air or missile attack. Like the network of evacuation tunnels that underlies much of Peking, and presumably other cities, this gives China a much more confident defensive posture.[17]

Goals of Education

Mao stressed the importance of the Cadre School (or farm) to bring white-collar personnel, administrators and educators closer to understanding the villagers by rotating time spent for farm work and Mao study. Government officials and college faculty spend a portion of each year at the farms, where they haul manure and work the fields to "reintegrate with the masses." More and more universities have reopened. An impact of the Cultural Revolution, academic work is being combined vigorously with labor and practical experience, through the introduction of industrial workshops at most schools and the requirement that students spend part of each year working on a farm commune or in a factory.[18]

Jonathan Mirsky writes that lack of success in some areas and questionable goals in others do not detract from the innovative and creative aspects of China's present orientation in the direction of elimination of competition and encouragement of mutual aid. Mirsky acknowledges the greatest achievement of the Cultural Revolution as the primary stress on work as an educational and transformational force, and not merely work, but work accompanied by study which leads to personal, social and political awareness.[19]

Family Structure

Parents and children live and eat together, sleep in their own house and cook in their own kitchen. But the family is no longer an enterprise, and it no longer has an estate to pass on. It is now a unit of residence, consumption, and child-rearing, like in our own society. Children are expected to support their aged parents, but old people with no adult children will be looked after by their team or brigade. They do not have to have large families and marry their children off as soon as possible. In fact, a family with a few unmarried adult children bringing in work points will probably enjoy the highest possible income of its team. This family can buy expensive consumer goods like a bicycle or a radio, or it can put its extra money into the local branch of the People's Bank at four percent annual interest and eventually use the savings to rebuild or improve the family home.[20]

There are pressures to distribute burdens equally and taxes and quotas tend to remain at the same levels over time. If a brigade or commune increases its production, it can keep the surplus and do whatever it pleases with it. From the ordinary worker on the land to the manager of the brigade with his office, files and telephones, life has become more susceptible to budgeting and calculation.

To a large extent social mobility now takes the form of working one's way up within an organization, of moving into a higher job classification, or of acquiring specialized skills that will result in a new and more responsible position within the organization.

Israel attracts attention because her right to existence has been disputed since the first day of independence. Acceptance by the community of nations was crucial to her survival. She has shown she has the capacity to defend herself successfully and in a like manner is making her own contribution to the world community. Her ties to the Third World occupied a major place in her foreign relations.[21]

Laufer calls attention to the fact that it was in line with Israel's basic policy goal of seeking the recognition of the world community that establishing contacts with ex-colonial countries was a political necessity.[22] What seems equally important is Israel's success in fashioning in a comparatively brief period of time a modern economy, a fairly-well integrated society and a social system in which cooperative and socialist principles of organization and distribution play an important role. For example, Tanzania requested Israel to provide a special training program in agricultural cooperation in connection with the desire of Tanzania to establish new forms of cooperative agricultural settlements. Israel was the only free world country to which Tanzania looked for instruction in this area. The interest in the Israeli-supported program of activities with developing countries derives from the Israeli agricultural and cooperative achievements. During 1970, more than 40 percent of the trainees coming to Israel received instruction in agricultural or cooperative practices and one third of the expert assignments were in those specialties.[23]

Political Structure

Israel's chief lawmaking body is the Knesset, a 120-member unicameral legislature elected by universal suffrage under proportional representation for four years, but which may, by specific legislation, decide on new elections before the end of its term. The Knesset has included representatives from nine or more parties, the largest controlling more than 38 percent of the seats. Since a government must be supported by a majority of Knesset members in order to survive, all of Israel's governments have been coalitions, based on compromise among several parties. The Cabinet, headed by the Prime Minister is collectively responsible to the Knesset. It takes office on receiving a vote of confidence from the Knesset and continues in office until after its resignation, the resignation (or death) of the Prime Minister or a vote of non-confidence—then a new one is constituted. As no party has so far commanded an absolute majority, all Cabinets have been based on coalitions.[24]

When the election returns are in, the leader of the largest party is invited to form a government. It is the leader of that party who conducts the coalition negotiation. In the recent election it was the Likud Party which was victorious and whose leader, Menachen Begin, emerged as the Prime Minister.

Infrastructure

Political movements and parties: Political movements and parties themselves are among the most important subcultural groupings in the Israel society. On May 17, 1977, Israel's governing Labor Party was defeated in the national parliamentary elections by the Lukud bloc, which, after twenty-five years as gadfly opposition, suddenly became the nation's leading political party. The election gave Likud 40 seats, the Labor Alignment 34, Democrat Movement for Change 14, National Religious Party 12, Agudat Israel and Poalei Agudat 5, Democrat Front (including Communists) 6, Shelli 2, Shlomzion 2, Shumel Flatto-Sharon 1, Independent Liberal Party 1, Citizens Rights Movement 1, and United Arab Party 1. Mapai, the Israel Labor Party, has a dominent voice in many quasi-governmental and extragovernmental institutions, such as the Jewish Agency, which handles most of the problems associated with immigration, and the Histradut, Israel's mammoth labor union.[25]

Political movements in Israel own or sponsor newspapers, publishing houses, youth movements, banks, insurance firms, agricultural settlements, housing projects, and educational institutions. Though exact figures on party membership are not available, about 40 percent of the adult population is formally enrolled in one party or another, and each one of the nine major parties is a mass party.[26] As a movement, it seeks to recruit as many members as possible, and to involve its members in as elaborate a network of intraparty relationships as possible.

Ben-Gurion as a Unifying Force

The transformation of Israel's voluntary, semi-professional and highly politicized security organizations into a unified, compulsory, professional and depoliticized army was accomplished by the determination and skill of David Ben-Gurion who took over the defense portfolio in June 1947. As Premier and Defense Minister from 1947 to 1963, Ben-Gurion stamped his indelible mark on both the army and Defense Ministry. More than any other factors, his personality and nationalist vision shaped the course of civil-military relations.[27] The institutionalized concepts and procedures initiated by Ben-Gurion include: 1) the nationalization, formalization and depoliticization of the army; 2) the supremacy of civilian authorities in determining the issues of war and peace; 3) the Defense Minister as the final arbiter of conflicts between civilians and the military; 4) a highly centralized decision-making process in matters of defense and related foreign policy issues limited to a small and highly cohesive civilian and military group, selected and dominated by the Defense Minister.[28] The type of authority which Ben-Gurion exercised in relation to his subordinates would be defined by Weber as charismatic authority.

Zahal—a professional unified depoliticized Army

The creation of Zahal from the Haganah illustrates how a colonizing movement and a society of social mission, predominantly maintained with primary, non-formalized groups, were transformed into formal bureaucratic structures. S. N. Eisenstadt holds that "all this did not give rise to a pure Weberian type of neutral bureaucracy. The non-bureaucratic elements existed not only on the top, directive levels . . . but became strongly interwoven also at other levels.'"[29] The organization of Zahal corrobates all aspects of this change: from voluntary to compulsory social and political action; from non-formal to formal organization; and intervention of non-bureaucratic elements at all levels.

Zahal's participation in nation building was dictated by Israel's special needs, demanding a pioneer army, one not bound by routine military functions, but an army fulfilling national building functions. From its creation, Ben Gurion had assigned to Zahal many of the functions formerly performed exclusively by pioneers. In taking on these tasks, the army assumed the pioneer image as well. Thus the esprit du corps of Zahal was nourished by the "pioneer legacy" of the past. Zahal's educational activities can be broken down into two main areas: 1) information, indoctrination and programs aimed at strengthening the civil and national consciousness; and 2) preparation to ready soldiers and officers for smooth integration into the society upon completion of military service. In 1952 a military specialization program was proposed to complement the humanities, science and agriculture programs already existing in the high schools. This effort was tied in with the formation of a military academy connected with Israel's foremost high schools, the Reali Gymnasium in Haifa and the Herzelia Gymnasium in Tel Aviv.

The Army as Agents of Socialization

In the government's effort at socialization, the army has been assigned special and major responsibility. Also, because Israel has universal military training for both men and women, the army is the most direct means of reaching all the young adults. An important area of its special responsibility has included its socializing work of new immigrants in the civilian population, from teaching elementary health care and diet habits, language and civics, sponsorship of language classes for the general population in addition to its training its young recruits and joint service in the army and on border kibbutzim.

Because Zahal is a people's army and a reserve organization, the barrack life is short; the officers are permanently integrated with society and the chances of officers becoming ideologically or professionally independent are minimal. The high requirements for efficiency and merit in Zahal makes the retired young officers a most desirable element in the civilian society. Zahal's graduates are achievement-oriented, and they are pragmatic, experienced managers. Consequently, all sectors of the society compete for the politically neutral and administration-oriented Zahal officers.

Nahal: Zahal's Special Army Unit (Fighting Youth Movement)

Nahal, the Fighting Youth Movement, was created in the spirit of the old agricultural pioneer settlements which regarded the kibbutz as an instrument to conquer the land. Nahal carries on the tradition of farmer-soldiers, working in border kibbutzim while serving in the army. Some kibbutzim are Nahal creations. Frequently the servicemen remain in the border collective settlements (usually on the most sensitive spots at the Syrian or Egyptian borders) they have helped establish after discharge from the service. The Nahal currently played a key role in settling the Israel-occupied territories in the Golan Heights and in Northern Sinai.

The Nahal program is composed of volunteers recruited mainly from the collective and cooperative agricultural settlements and from the pioneer Socialist Youth Movements in the cities.[30]

Relationship between the Military and Civil Power—Its Involvement in Nation-Building and Economic Modernization

Zahal's extra military functions, those activities not directly related to warfare, are a critical aspect of civil-military relations in

Israel. In developing states, breakdowns in modernization, an uneven development in social and political mobilization or inadequate integration have often created situations where the army must assume the tasks of managing and directing economic, agricultural and educational enterprises. In such situations, the army usually intervenes because of the absence, importance or indifference of other elites. In Israel, however, there was no such modernization breakdown. The task of modernizing and integrating fell upon civilian organizations and the army simply complemented their work.

In Israel there is a reasonable and well-established reciprocity between the civilian stratification, economic, and political systems and the social and stratification systems of the army. In other words, the exchange of goods, services, and skills between these two sectors and the revolution in modern military doctrines has closed the gap between these two sectors. This is so for the following reasons: (a) The rate of technological change has accelerated and a wider diversity of skill is required to maintain the military establishment, and (b) the diversification and specialization of military technology have lengthened the time of formal training required for mastery of military technology, with the result that the temporary citizen army becomes less important and the completely professional army more vital.[31]

Perlmutter explains that role expansion represents the equilibrium achieved by Zahal between its strictly professional functions and the voluntaristic legacy of its pioneer forerunners. The transfer of the functions of a mission-oriented community to a military apparatus and its bureaucratic structures and the interplay of two opposing orientations—professional versus voluntaristic attitudes—shaped this army in a way which could not have been predicted by either orientation.[32]

The Contribution of the Kibbutz

In Israel there are more than 200 kibbutzim, containing 3.2

percent of the country's people. Here children are raised not in the home of their parents, but in a communal house with other children their own age. From infancy on, they sleep, eat and study in these special children's homes. They spend several hours each day with their parents, and there is no effort to deny the natural family. The peer group however appears to be more influential than the family. The experiences of communal living with its implicit ideological lessons is easily supplemented by an educational program which stresses the values and ideology of the Kibbutz. Kibbutz children therefore are much more ideologically oriented than their urban contemporaries.[33]

The kibbutzim encourage their young men to volunteer for training as pilots, paratroopers, or other elite military occupations. While the collective settlements are no more than 4% of Israel's populations, 25% of the total killed and wounded Zahal officers were from the kibbutzim.[34]

1963-1965 Conscripts: Rate of Basic Qualification and Career Mobility in Percentages*

Rate of Basic Qualification	Sons of Kibbutzim	Others
1 (highest)	69	23
2	43	21
3	39	28
4	51	24
5	32	19
6	22	8
7 (lowest)	33	3

*Intelligence, education, knowledge of Hebrew, personal qualifications, and country of birth.

Fitness for Command Position
Among Zahal's Conscripts in Percentages

Fitness	1961-2 Conscripts			1963-4 Conscripts		
	Sons of Kibbutz	Educated in Kibbutz	Others	Sons of Kibbutz	Educated in Kibbutz	Others
High	60	50	46	65	52	54
Medium	21	20	31	12	22	14
Low	19	30	23	23	26	32

Table 11, p. 257
Source: Y. Amir, "Sons of Kibbutzim in Zahal," Magamot, Vol. 15 No. 203 (August 1967).[55]

Israel and the Agricultural Revolution

Israel's agricultural revolution came about by the application of science and technology. Impetus has come from Israel's various technical and scientific institutions spearheaded by the Weizman Institute for Science, the Haifa Technion and the Levi Eshkol School of Agriculture.

The creation of irrigation networks has changed the whole pattern of agriculture. Intensive farming, based on planned use of water, became far more important than extensive farming, with the farmer relying on rainfall from the skies. Land use is not left to the whim of the farmer, but is carefully planned, so that today every gallon of water and every acre of land gives optimum results. Mechanization, the use of fertilizers, genetic improvement of livestock and seeds, pest control and the eradication of livestock diseases—all these have been achieved through a partnership between farmers and scientists.

Agriculture is the largest sector of the labor economy and in terms of social value has made the most original contribution. The kibbutz and moshav are essentially part of the labor movement. Both are based on the principles of national land, self labor, mutual aid and cooperation. The kibbutz cultivates all its land communally for the benefit of the group as a whole. The moshav consists of small holdings cultivated independently by each family. There are also villages, known as moshavin shitufin, which combine features of the two. Over 90% of all kibbutzim and the great majority of moshavim are affiliated with the Histradut or General Federation of Labor, the largest and most representative labor movement in Israel. It has no ideological criterion of membership, but is open to working people of every trade and profession, of all political and religious views, who join on a direct, individual basis. Politics enter it through the General Convention, chosen once in about 4 years in direct voting by the total membership on lists of candidates linked with political parties. Histradut decisions largely reflect Mapai policy. The Histradut has four principal activities: trade unionism, health and welfare, education and economics. Histradut is at one and the same time a federation of trade unions, an association of social welfare organizations, an educational agency, and a holding company of economic undertakings.[36]

What Assessment Can Be Made of the Study of the Two Societies, The People's Republic of China and Israel under Comparison?

I have accepted Lipset's caution for the need of some systematic way to be used in comparing national values. I am also reminded of Parson's pattern variables, achievement—ascription, universalism—particularism, and specificity—diffuseness. Lipset adds an equalitarian elitist distinction: that a society's values may stress that all persons must be respected because they are human beings, or it may emphasize the general superiority of those who hold elite positions. That is, in an equalitarian society, the differences between low-status and high-status people are thought to be accidental and perhaps temporary variations in position, differences which should not be stressed in social relations, and which do not convey to the high status person a general claim to social deference. By contrast, in an elitist society those holding high positions in any structure, whether business, in intellectual activities, or in government, are thought to deserve respect and deference. Especially significant is the fact that from a comparative perspective the values prevalent in a nation at any given time condition the reaction with which the historical struggle is played out.[37]

In Communist China as in Israel, a parliamentary democracy, both societies function as group and community oriented, in a highly ideological frame of reference. Politically different, both countries have a strong sense of national purpose. To this commitment there exists the "messianic visionary," there is a sense of coherence, collective mission.[38] This is reflected in both societies by strong social cohesion. Both nations, while committed to peace, feel their survival is being threatened, consequently there is a need for preparedness at all times against the possibility of attack.

Family lifestyle reflects ideological orientation whether it is in the structure of the Kibbutz child-rearing institution or demonstrated by the cohesive bonds of the Productive Teams of the Chinese Communist society. In the case of the Kibbutz, however, the members are free to leave. To keep the younger people in the Kibbutz, the government has encouraged the training in the areas of science and technology which has great appeal for this group.

While both nations identify themselves as non-militaristic, both the P.L.A. and the Zahal have played a distinctive role in the socialization process. In China after the cultural revolution, the People's Liberation Army played a strong part in moving the society towards Thermidor. The influence of the army is still felt in all areas, government, industry and in the schools. In Israel, since its inception Zahal has played a vital role in the socialization process, teaching the language, providing the moral training and in training its Youth Group, Nahal.

Both Communist China and Israel can fit in neatly with Weber's theory of growing bureaucracy as modernization in the society takes firm hold. For the present, Communist China appears to feel tight control over the elite bureaucratic structure is crucial to retaining the mass line, and it will retain the constant struggle with the vertical power structure feeding down to the lower hierarchy, for the redefinition of the power struggle.

Israel, from the start, with the development of Zahal found itself the vehicle through its capacity to develop new institutional settings or structural framework. As for Histradut, from the earliest it was formidable in its capacity to supply the initiative needed to build the labor movement and project itself into the dynamics and bloodstream, pumping vitality into the society. The unique interplay and balance between army and civilian has also added to the stability of the nation. Critically, the role played by the political parties' coalition provide the viscosity for stability. Eisenstadt makes a useful point when he writes that modernization requires not only a relatively stable new structure but one capable of adapting to continuously changing conditions and problems. It has always been a revolutionary process of undermining and changing the existing institutional structure. The possibility of successful institutionalization of an innovating or revolutionary process is never inherent in the revolutionary act itself. It depends on other conditions, primarily the society's capacity for internal transformation.[39] Israel has demonstrated by innovation and capacity for change and growth that her present system, a parliamentary democracy strengthened by the role played by the coalition of the political parties, provides the necessary structural framework for her political stability for the present.

On the other hand, totalitarianism came to Communist China under circumstances of economic, social and political instability, generated by years of exploitation from within. Following the

Cultural Revolution, the People's Liberation Army was called in to help restore order. Pragmatism is the position today with the emphasis that once the production team meets the state grain quota they be allowed to earn more money. With the death of Mao Tse-tung, power is currently shared by a triumvirate of Chairman Hua Kuo-feng, and two vice chairmen, Yeh Chien-ying, the aged Defense Minister, and Teng Hsiao-ping, the elderly Deputy Prime Minister. Teng Hsiao-ping has emerged as China's guiding force from the recently concluded 11th Congress and it is felt that Teng with his experience will be an important influence in putting the country back into shape. Most of the new directions Peking is now taking, the stress on profits and production in industry, the return to a more conventional educational system, the upgrading of the role of science and technology, were presaged in Government documents prepared by Mr. Teng in 1975 before he was ousted as a rightist.

The 11th Congress elected a new leadership heavily weighted towards the bureaucrats Mao purged in the Cultural Revolution, senior military officers and technocrats. In contrast to the one elected in 1973, the new 26-member Politburo contains not a single representative from the groups Mao sought to promote in the Cultural Revolution to preserve China's revolutionary vigor. The new party constitution adopted by the Congress enshrines some of the new leaders' differences with Mao. While pledging to uphold his policies, the constitution stipulates that the Communist Party is now responsible for insuring that China becomes a powerful Socialist country with a modern agriculture, industry, national defense and science and technology by the turn of the century.[40]

Stressing rapid economic growth at this time, China's practical new leaders are studying Yugoslav's system of worker self-management with a view to motivating workers towards increasing production output. Exactly how power is shared among China's top leaders is speculative with little substantive evidence to go on.

The Party Congress did offer one clue; Mr. Yeh, who is regarded as something of an Elder Statesman, a man whose long revolutionary experience puts him in the vintage of Mao and the late Chou En-lai, told the delegates that "Chairman Hua can certainly lead our Party, our army and the people of all nationalities triumphantly into the 21st century."

Both Israel and Communist China are a party to the Agricultural Revolution in their own individual fashion, Israel with its mechanization, use of fertilizers, genetic improvement of livestock and Communist China with its own method of enrichening the soil and better crop control.

If the Chinese philosophy is a continual process of re-education and if something can be added concerning the Chinese, it is that they must be understood in terms of making their system work for them. John Kenneth Galbraith explains that "the Chinese economy is not the American or European future. But it is the Chinese future, and let there be no doubt, for the Chinese it works."[41]

Is there any evidence to support the notion that totalitarianism is indigenous to some particular stratum of society, in particular totalitarianism of the "left?" Lipset does find a link between totalitarianism and social class but the pattern requires further differentiation. Lipset finds that, among major types of totalitarianism, each has its own distinctive socioeconomic base of support. The communist version of totalitarianism finds the following among the lower classes while the Fascist and Nazi appeal can be identified with the middle class. In the lower class, Lipset has identified first a basic predisposition toward authoritarianism—a latent congeniality toward totalitarian values. But the basic predisposition toward authoritarianism of which Lipset speaks suggests that only some circumstances of extreme stress may be necessary to activate the latent tendencies. In that event, the economic interests of the lower class might easily find expression in a totalitarianism of the "left."[42]

BIBLIOGRAPHY

Barnett, A. Doak, Ed. *Chinese Politics in Action*. Seattle: University of Washington Press, 1969.

Barnett, A. Doak. With a contribution by Ezra Vogel. *Cadres, Bureaucracy, and Political Power in Communist China*. New York: Columbia University Press, 1967.

Butterfield, Fox, "China's Leadership: The Right Wing," The New York Times, August 28, 1977, section 4, 2.

Cohen, Ronald and Middleton, John, Eds. *Comparative Political Systems*. S. N. Eisenstadt, "Transformation of Social, Political and Cultural Orders in Modernization," Garden City, New York: The Natural History Press, 1967.

De Glopper, Donald R. "Recent Changes in Chinese Society," *The Annals of the American Academy of Political and Social Science, China in the World Today*. July, 1972, 402, 9.

Enzel, Alan. "Totalitarian Ideologies," in collaboration with Reom Christensen, Dan N. Jacobs, Mostafa Rejai and Herbert Waltzer. *Ideologies and Modern Politics*. New York: Dodd, Mead & Co., 1971, 54-55.

Fairbanks, John N. "The New China and the American Connection," *Foreign Affairs*. October, 1972, 51:5, 31.

Fein, Leonard J. *Israel Politics and People*. Boston: Little, Brown & Company, 1967.

Galbraith, John Kenneth. "Galbraith Has Seen China's Future, and It Works," *The New York Times Magazine*. November 26, 1972, 101.

Gayn, Mark. "Who After Mao," *Foreign Affairs*. January, 1973, 51:2, 302, 303.

Goode, William J., Ed. *The Dynamics of Modern Society*. Seymour Martin Lipset, "The Value Patterns of Democracy: A Case Study in Comparative Analysis," New York: Atherton Press, 1966.

Harding, Harry. "Political Trends in China since the Cultural Revolution," *The Annals*, 77.

Hofheinz, Roy, Jr. "The Ecology of Chinese Communist Success: Rural Influence Patterns," *Chinese Communist Politics in Action*. Ed. by A. Doak Barnett, Seattle: University of Washington Press, 1969.

Kau, Yang-Mao. "The Urban Bureaucratic Elite in Communist China: A Case Study of Wuhan, 1949-65." *Chinese Communist Politics in Action*. Ed. by A. Doak Barnett. Seattle: University of Washington Press, 1969.

Laufer, Leopold. "Israel and the Third World," *Political Science Quarterly*. December, 1972. LXXXVII:4, 616.

Meir, Ziona. "The Labor Movement," Israel Today, Jerusalem: Israel Digest, 1965.

Perlmutter, Amos. *Military and Politics in Israel*. New York: Frederick A. Praeger, Inc., 1969.

Phillips, Warren H. "A Move to Moderation on Almost Every Level Permeates the Nation," *The Wall Street Journal*. October 30, 1972, 18.

Rejai, Mostafa. "Guerrilla Communism, China, North Vietnam, Cuba," with the collaboration of Rheom Christensen, Alan S. Enzel, Dan N. Jacobs and Herbert Waltzer. *Ideologies and Modern Politics*. New York: Dodd, Mead & Co., 1971, 152-153.

Tuchman, Barbara. "Friendship with Foreign Devils," *Harper's*. December, 1972, 245:1471, 50.

FOOTNOTES

[1] A. Doak Barnett, ed., *Chinese Communist Politics in Action*, Seattle: University of Washington Press, 1969, introduction XII.

[2] John N. Fairbank, "The New China and the American Connection," *Foreign Affairs*, October, 1972, 51:5, 31.

[3] Mostafa Rejai, "Guerrilla Communism, China, North Vietnam, Cuba," with the collaboration of Rheo M. Christenson, Alan S. Engel, Dan N. Jacobs and Herbert Waltzer, *Ideologies and Modern Politics*, New York: Dodd, Mead & Co., 1971, 152-153.

[4] Warren H. Phillips, "A Move to Moderation On Almost Every Level Permeates the Nation," *The Wall Street Journal*, October 30, 1972, 18.

[5] A. Doak Barnett, with a contribution by Ezra Vogel, *Cadres, Bureaucracy, and Political Power in Communist China*, New York: Columbia University Press, 1967, 427-429.

[6] Yang-Mao Kau, "The Urban Bureaucratic Elite in Communist China: A Case Study of Wuhan, 1949-65," A. Doak Barnett, ed., *China Communist Politics in Action*, Seattle: University of Washington Press, 1969, 216.

[7] *Ibid.*, 219.

[8] Barnett, 433.

[9] Barnett, 435.

[10] Barnett, 437.

[11] Donald R. De Glopper, "Recent Changes in Chinese Society," *The Annals of The American Academy of Political and Social Science, China in the World Today*, July, 1972, 402, 9.

[12] De Glopper, 22.

[13] Barnett, 444.

[14] Barbara Tuchman, "Friendship with Foreign Devils," *Harper's*, December, 1972, 245:1471, 50.

[15] Warren H. Phillips, "A Move to Moderation on Almost Every Level Permeates the Nation," *The Wall Street Journal*, October 30, 1972, 1.

[16] Harry Harding, "Political Trends in China since the Cultural Revolution," *The Annals*, 77.

[17] Fairbanks, 34.

[18] Phillips, 18.

[19] Jonathan Mirsky, "China After Nixon," *The Annals*, 83, 90.

[20]DeGlopper, 19, 20.
[21]Leopold Laufer, "Israel and the Third World," *Political Science Quarterly*, December, 1972, LXXXVII:4, 616.
[22]*Ibid*.
[23]*Ibid*., 621.
[24]Leonard J. Fein, *Israel Politics and People*, Boston: Little, Brown & Co., 1967, 37.
[25]*Ibid*., 38.
[26]*Ibid*., 89.
[27]Amos Perlmutter, *Military and Politics in Israel*, New York: Frederick A. Praeger, Inc., 1969, 54.
[28]*Ibid*., 55.
[29]Perlmutter, 63, from S. N. Eisenstadt, *Israel*, 427.
[30]Perlmutter, 72.
[31]Perlmutter, 69.
[32]*Ibid*., 78.
[33]Fein, 150.
[34]Perlmutter, 62.
[35]Perlmutter, 63.
[36]Ziona Meir, "The Labor Movement," *Israel Today*, Jerusalem: Israel Digest, 1965, 18.
[37]William J. Goode, ed., *The Dynamics of Modern Society*, Seymour Martin Lipset, "The Value Patterns of Democracy: A Case Study in Comparative Analysis, New York: Atherton Press, 1966, 255.
[38]Hofheinz, 3.
[39]Ronald Cohen and John Middleton, Eds., *Comparative Political Systems*, S. N. Eisenstadt, "Transformation of Social, Political and Cultural Orders in Modernization," Garden City, New York: The Natural History Press, 1967, 439, 440.
[40]Fox Butterfield, "China's Leadership: The Right Wing," *The New York Times*, August 28, 1977, section 4, 2.
[41]John Kenneth Galbraith, "Galbraith Has Seen China's Future, and It Works," *The New York Times Magazine*, November 26, 1972, 101.
[42]Alan Enzel, "Totalitarian Ideologies," in collaboration with Reom Christensen, Dan J. Jacobs, Mostafa Rejai, and H. Waltzer, *Ideologies & Modern Politics*, New York: Mead & Co., 1971, 54, 55.

The Community College: Issues & Priorities for the 70s

Two decades ago Richard Hofstader wrote that "a new institution, the community college, has sprung up in large numbers to meet the demand for something like mass education beyond the normal four year secondary school."[1]

Professor Arthur M. Cohen of the Graduate School of the University of California at Los Angeles describes it as one of the unique accomplishments of American education in the twentieth century. As such it represents expanded educational opportunity for all because it offers the vehicle by means of which the nation is accelerating the pursuit of its educational ideal. Cohen feels that it should not be considered an extension of secondary school, it has broader purposes and a different student population. It can best be described as becoming the vehicle providing all youth with an opportunity to obtain an education and training to the best of their capabilities. That is its unique mission.[2] For Medsker and Tillery, the "college for the community" is a phenomenon of this decade.[3]

In their 1972 report the Carnegie Commission on Higher Education, "The Campus and the City," in emphasizing that improving the capabilities of our colleges to serve urban needs are tasks of the highest priority, has assigned to the community colleges the major responsibility for increasing initial access to higher education, and providing a wide range of vocational and occupational programs. The Commission points out that the "land-grant movement was one of the most revolutionary ideas in the history of higher education." It provided the momentum for the development of colleges with a new sense of direction to the needs of a dominant force in American society at that time—rural America, and today we need a similar commitment to direct the attention of our colleges to the concern of urban America.

The community college is viewed as playing a crucial role in this current movement. Based on enrollment estimates to 1980, the Commission sees the need for the establishment of some 175 to 235 additional two-year community colleges with from 80 to 125 of these colleges to be established in metropolitan areas with a population in excess of 500,000. The final report of the Commission for 1973 "Priorities for Action" suggests more faculty consultation on urban, as there was years ago on rural, problems. The Commission also recommends a wider spread of community colleges across the nation with their cultural and adult education programs so that 95 percent of all persons will be within commuting distance of a college.[4]

Ten years ago, one out of five students in the nation began his work in a community college. Now, the number is more than one out of three. Soon, it will be one out of two.[5]

America's community colleges mean many things.... For some, they may mean the best, if not the only hope for educational experience beyond the high school. For others, they may represent the best means to a baccalaureate degree and perhaps eventual graduate study in a professional field.... For still others, the community college may mean the chance for experience and training that will lead to satisfying jobs in a wide range of fields.

The public two-year community colleges come in all shapes and sizes. Some are located in the heart of great urban centers, some in rural communities, many in small towns across the country. While they may differ in size and scope of operations, they have one characteristic in common. They represent "opportunity" for the many as well as the few. Cities, towns, rural communities and counties have fastened onto the concept of the community college as a means of extending and expanding educational opportunity. Developing public interest in alleviating social and economic problems as well as insuring that everybody gets a chance for higher education has resulted in its rapid growth. There are some 700 community colleges now in operation. As many as 50 have been established in a recent year. The rate of growth is expected to continue as more and more communities turn to this kind of institution for educational expansion.

The comprehensive or multipurpose community college appears to fit a great variety of needs of the American community. By 1980 enrollment is expected to exceed 4 million. What is most significant is that many students who only a decade ago would not have considered going beyond high school now tend to continue their education. This has led to a great diversity among students and among programs.[6]

Factors that make the comprehensive community college the most significant of all higher institutions in extending educational opportunities include: 1) low cost; 2) location close to home; 3) non-selective admissions policy; 4) tendency to offer a variety of programs in government, business, health fields, many of which lead directly to employment; 5) work study, where students spend half of their time in the classroom and the other half on the job, seeing the practical application of their theoretical study; 6) offering large numbers from lower socio economic levels opportunities to continue their education and upgrade their abilities by counseling and remedial care; 7) by its non traditional approach, offering a variety of programs which can give many a "second chance"; 8) increasing numbers of adults at all levels who wish to enhance their personal competence; 9) community service.[7]

Because of its comprehensiveness, there is something for everyone. For the aspiring and qualified student, that may be a preprofessional course of study that will lead to transfer to a four-year college. To help students make the right choices, there are expert counseling and guidance staffs who assist them in selecting a program, whether it is one that may lead to transfer or one that results in a position in one of the many occupational fields.

Career Students

It is estimated that there are over 20,000 occupational education programs in community colleges in the country. The scope of career training is enormous. Students in these programs are prepared for technical work or supervisory jobs in government, business and industry, health fields and in such new areas as environmental control technology. A typical community college offers career courses in nursing, supervisory and administrative management, chemical technology, interior design, fire science, law enforcement, food service management, accounting, child services, secretarial practices, and data processing. Community colleges try to offer training in fields where people are needed, for example, the expanding health care field. They also train medical assistants, x-ray technicians, dental aides and office managers. Career courses also tend to reflect local needs. A San Francisco or Miami two-year college will offer training for careers in the motel and restaurant business that abounds in those areas. A community college in Montana offers training to young men who will go into the lumber business. A Kansas two-year college offers courses in feed yard technology, meat inspection and animal hospital technology. In South Carolina a junior college gives training for the textile industry. In the work-study program, students spend half their time in the classroom and the other half on the job. A student may study educational psychology in the classroom mornings, and work with children in a day-care center in the afternoons. Another may take pre-law courses half the week and spend the other half working in an attorney's office. The practitioner is sought in almost all of the career courses. Attorneys in the community are sought to teach some of the pre-law courses; physicians, dentists and nurses to teach courses in the health field; businessmen, accountants and office managers to share their practical know how with students.[8]

Adult Courses

Students see their parents returning to college to catch up with new discoveries in technology. Older women whose families are now grown, come to college for the first time to prepare for a middle-years career. In the 1960's police departments began exploring how nearby two-year colleges could serve them by working out short courses. For example, policemen would come to the campuses for a few weeks to take a course in psychology of mobs. It was found that such a course changed the way policemen dealt with crowds and gave them a better understanding of the sociological problem that caused riots. The "CAPP" Program (the College Accelerated Program for Police) government-supported at low tuition ($15.00 per credit), social-science oriented, illustrates both the need and desire of "educational mobility," to fit in with a complex, dynamic and fast-moving society.[9]

Cost

The cost of college is a very real consideration for most students. Tuition and fees at public two-year colleges average about $250.00 a year. Arizona, California and Wisconsin are tuition free for residents. In addition, many of the New York City and Chicago community colleges are free. The goal of the two-year college movement is to put campuses within commuting range of every college-age student. That goal is much closer to realization than was ever thought possible. California, Wisconsin, Florida, Illinois, North Carolina, Ohio, Texas, Pennsylvania and New York have nearly accomplished that aim.[10]

Student Body

Medsker and Tillery point out that the student body of most community colleges is not composed only of those on the lower end of the various scales. The typical community college tends to draw heavily from all quartiles of ability distribution. In terms of general background, the composition of the student body is highly representative of the community as a whole.[11]

Guidance

Medsker's recent study of junior colleges shows that 2/3 of the faculty members recognize guidance as an integral part of the educational programs in their college. Guidance services are provided both by professional counselors and by members of the faculty. The Carnegie study of guidance in 2-year colleges showed that the recommended ratio of 1 to 300 is only achieved exceptionally. It is expected that soon there will be as many adult students in junior colleges as there are youth immediately out of high school. The implication of this for guidance programs are profound since only a few junior colleges now have older students, and many do not even have regular counseling services available for the thousands of adults in the evening divisions. Guidance is expected to assume increasing importance as the community colleges continue to emphasize the educability of all students, the exploration of opportunity, and the development of individual interests and talents.[12]

Control and Support

Today there are two basic state patterns that prevail: 1) responsibility for the community college is shared between local and state government; 2) this responsibility rests primarily with the state. The trend is in the direction of greater state control over public higher education. Where there is full state control, there are strong local advisory committees with responsibility for making recommendations to both the college and state board, and the involvement of college administrators and faculty in state planning and policy making have helped to retain local initiative.[13]

The community college movement has also been described as part of a revolution growing out of the realization of the need for solutions other than traditional to meet present societal needs. Basic to the concept is the fact that 1) the community college is centered within a community; 2) it represents a shift of emphasis from a single purpose to a multi purpose institution; 3) it is unique in that it embraces two years of college work, has features such as transfer and selected occupational programs, and 4) it is the fastest-growing educational institution devoted to the fulfillment of certain broad but identifiable educational purposes.[14]

Up to the time he took over as president of newly created Berkshire Community College, Thomas O'Connell explained, "There were lots of people like me who had no idea what this new kind of college was all about. Sometimes described as a uniquely American or democratic institution, it recognizes the importance of the average person's having the opportunity to go beyond high school. Actually it is this multi-purpose quality which accounts for the growing popularity of the community college."[15]

Evolution of the Community College

Historically, the junior colleges evolved from the egalitarian premise that educationally the individual should be allowed to develop the limits of his capabilities. The movement made progress under William Rainey Harper, President of the University of Chicago at the turn of the century, who set up a system of affiliated colleges attached to an academy or public high school. In 1911 in

Fresno, California the high school established a junior college with three teachers and 15 students. New York, Oklahoma and Mississippi were early in establishing state supported systems of public junior colleges, primarily to provide opportunities for rural youth. Implementation of the comprehensive community college was stimulated and fostered by the Smith Hughes vocational legislation in the 1920s and the pressing economic needs growing out of the Depression.[16]

President Truman's Commission on Higher Education recommended several measures for improving opportunities for a college education but the one measure which was offered most vigorously was the development of the tuition-free community college—extending the public schools to grades thirteen and fourteen. It was felt that the democratic community cannot tolerate a society based upon education for the well to do alone. Aptly stated by Gleazer, "in a democratic nation which holds that any citizen can be President or can achieve greater status than his father, education is the means. Thus educational opportunity is more than a privilege; it is a citizen's right."[17] The Eisenhower administration also encouraged the expansion of the community colleges as returning veterans of both World War II and, even more recently, the Vietnam war sought educational avenues for training to move up. Included also in this movement were adults who before had never considered college, and even more recently minority groups, the urban disadvantaged and other poverty groups who demanded equal educational opportunities as their "right."

Measurement of Growth

The increase in student enrollment in public community colleges has been spectacular. Combined full time and part-time enrollment in 1958, totaled 374,672. By 1968, that combined figure had increased almost 400%, to approximately 1,811,000. A more meaningful picture of enrollment growth in public colleges can be gained from a diachronic comparison of full-time with part time. Chart 3[18] shows that both categories of student enrollment have increased substantially since 1958—by 530 percent for parttime students and 340 percent for full-time students in 1967. Until 1965, part-time students outnumbered full-time by an annual average of approximately 55,000. Then in 1966, full-time enrollment for the first time surpassed by 38,000 the number of part-time students. This reversal appears to be a consistent trend. Medsker and Tillery point out that this general growth data can be understood in terms of a public growing increasingly aware of the need for acquiring skills and knowledge in a complex society. Recognition also is seen in terms of increasing need for local public institutions of higher education which can fill that need and at nominal cost. Between 1958 and 1968, technological and skilled manpower needs mandated the expansion of community college curricula. There was both increase in the number of institutions as well as new programs. The Vocational Education Act of 1963 and other enabling federal career legislation gave massive financial support for the widest array of occupational training programs. Since 1960, the upsurge has been marked in the number of students enrolled in programs which are credited towards the Bachelor's degree. In 1968 approximately 1/5 of degree credit enrollments were in the two year community colleges.[19]

As we move beyond the midpoint of the seventies, our focus is directed to a number of the broader issues facing community colleges: 1) minority access to college; 2) open admissions and realizable goals; 3) implementation of the egalitarian principle; 4) faculty commitment; 5) accountability; 6) what is their mission?

The 1971 Ford Foundation report stressed that education, and especially higher education, has functioned as the chief instrument of social mobility for every ethnic group in American society, except for ethnic groups that are not white. Thus the issue of minority access to college becomes one of the dominant issues of the 1970s. With the increased urbanization of Black Americans,

CHART 3

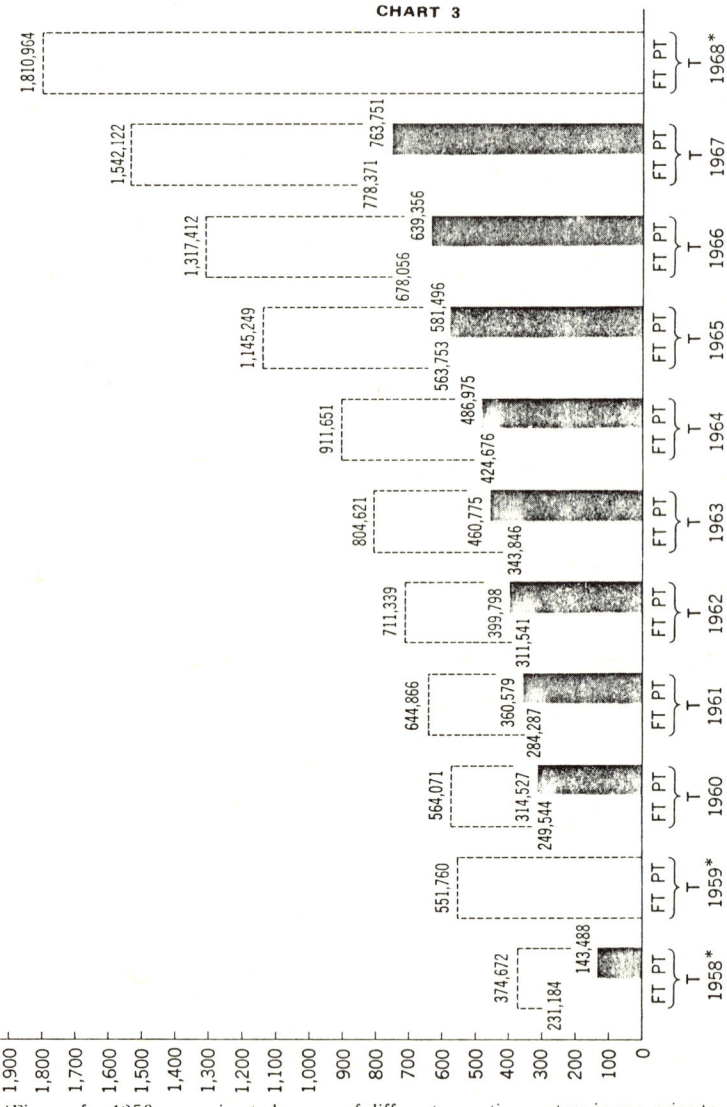

Year	FT	PT	Total
1958*	231,184	143,488	374,672
1959*			551,760
1960	249,544	314,527	564,071
1961	284,287	360,579	644,866
1962	311,541	399,798	711,339
1963	343,846	460,775	804,621
1964	424,676	486,975	911,651
1965	563,753	581,496	1,145,249
1966	678,056	639,356	1,317,412
1967	778,371	763,751	1,542,122
1968*			1,810,964

*Figures for 1958 approximate because of different reporting system in use prior to 1960. Figures for 1959 were not broken down into full- and part-time. Figures for 1968 are gross as full- and part-time breakdown was not available at time of publication. SOURCE: American Association of Junior Colleges annual directories.

Comparison of full- and part-time public community college enrollments, 1958-1968 the public, urban community colleges are expected to become the most important point for their entry into postsecondary education. Questions of public accountability enter as higher education comes to be considered a necessity for all.[20]

How can young persons of all talents and family incomes best be aided in getting a fair educational start into life and work? How might higher education make a greater contribution to the realization of equality of opportunity? These are among the priorities for action to which the Carnegie Commission addresses itself in its final report for 1973.

The Commission believes Higher Education has been given an increasing responsibility for the realization of equality of opportunity. Higher Education in 1870 enrolled 2 percent of the college age group; in 1970, it enrolled nearly 50 percent. In the Fall of 1972, blacks were represented among new enrollees in college in almost the same proportions as they were represented among high school graduates. The proportion 10 years ago was more nearly 2 to 3 than 1 to 1. The community colleges have been given an equal responsibility for their implementation of their program of open admissions. The commission has suggested creation of a sufficiency of open access, particularly at the lower division level, available at low or no tuition, within commuting distance for all. They are especially concerned with availability of open access in the metropolitan area.[21]

Open Admissions: What is the open door policy? Basically, it means any person who is a high school graduate, regardless of scholastic record, or anyone with a high school diploma can enroll. There is today widespread discussion and much difference of opinion about the principle of open enrollment in all institutions of higher education. Colleges as well as state governing boards throughout the country are grappling with the questions of how far to go in applying the concept. Medsker and Tillery feel it may be that it will be applied more within the total system of postsecondary education in each of the states than in individual institutions. Here it is felt the community college will play an increasingly important role in providing opportunities for all who wish to continue their education.[22]

Open admissions does not guarantee that a person will be admitted because he or she desires to enter that course or program. The college normally retains the right to place students in areas where there is evidence individuals have a reasonable chance of success. There is agreement that in order for the open door to be genuine there is need for several supporting policies among which is more financial aid to worthy students. Jencks and Riesman point out the sacrifice involved for many families in order to send their children to college. If the open door is not to become self-defeating, the community colleges will have to provide more counseling and direction to students. Monroe sees a need for more options, as well as a career ladder principle—to encourage development of potential for achievement to the highest possible degree, and a broadly based curriculum which combines skill development and academic studies.[23]

Access is not enough for the disadvantaged or minority student. In its report "A Chance to Learn" the Carnegie Commission addresses itself as to how Higher Education might meet this problem. They propose the adoption of a foundation year in which students are given intensive counseling and wide latitude to find a program that fits their interests and needs. They found the "greatest, single hurdle for the graduate of urban, lower-class high school is the equality of the education with which they emerge and their shaky mastery of skills and concepts essential to further learning." They also recommended that state planning agencies through metropolitan task forces study in depth the higher education resources available in their central cities to find ways to insure that at least 1 out of every 3 undergraduate student spaces in central cities be available on an open admission basis with either low tuition or effective student financial aid programs.[24]

The final report of the commission for 1973 indicates: a) There are new types of students, many of them drawn from among minorities and low income families, but more of them also from the more affluent classes. Many in the former group are more vocationally oriented and some in the latter group are more inclined toward political activity than have been most students in earlier times. b) There is also a new job market, more fluctuating in its specific demand for trained talent. The recommendation is for operation within a 2-year planning module with a degree available every two years and greater use of the Associate in Arts degree, including its use within 4-year colleges. In general, it has favored reform in three directions: toward more options for students in their attendance patterns; toward more diversity of programs both as among and within individual institutions, thus expanding the range of choice for students; and toward enrichment of programs. It sees the community college as living in both the worlds of higher education and of further education and constituting a connecting element between them. It is an expanding sector of Higher Education, with emphasis on serving the non-traditional more and also because it provides specific occupational skill training and experiential programs.[25]

The commission strongly supports the continuation of basic reliance on the states. The states must be prepared to spend an average of about 1.0 percent of per capita income on state support of Higher Education for the rest of this decade. Education must be adjusted to specific social needs. The commission feels Higher Education was underfunded. Federal assistance is recommended to equalize regional differences, as are the lowering of tuition in public colleges, with no tuition charged for the first 2 years, and an increased emphasis on adult education.

Community colleges, carefully planned on a state-by-state basis, should provide cultural and educational services to local communities. They should offer semi-professional and vocational programs including general education and their curricula should be regarded as terminal. Adult education should be of equal importance as traditional education in all institutions. A further recommendation is that each college and university should become a "community college" offering services to the local community. Asserting that the denial of educational opportunity sorely restricts the preparation of individuals for effective living, the commission concludes that "equal access to Higher Education must become one of the nation's highest priorities." This can only be realized if a concerted effort were made to eliminate economic barriers and discrimination, and to provide financial assistance to students and more educational opportunities for adults.[26]

More than 1/3 of all entering college students now begin their work in community colleges. For the country as a whole community college enrollment is about 8 percent of the 18-to-24-year-old population. By 1980 this may rise as high as 11 percent. This phenomenal development and potential for increased enrollment identifies it as the fastest growing segment of American education. The recent explosion in junior college enrollment has been largely confined to the pace-setter states: California, New York, Illinois, Michigan, Florida, Texas and Washington, which account for more than 2/3 of all enrollments in 1968 and over 1/3 of all public community colleges. Of the 739 public two-year colleges nationwide these 7 states have 286; of this latter number, 85 have opened since 1960. The public community college system of California now has nearly 100 institutions and leads the rest of the nation in enrollment. For the country as a whole, there has been a steady annual rise of about 1 percent in the proportion of total undergraduates attending junior colleges. It is anticipated that this rate of shift from four-to two-year institutions will continue during the coming decade. As this chart shows, whereas less than one fifth of undergraduates were in junior colleges in 1955, it is likely that by 1980 over one third of such undergraduates will be attending two-year colleges.[27]

As Medsker and Tillery point out, the community college appears to play two dominant roles: a) It serves an ever-increasing percentage of recent high school graduates who enter it expecting to continue later in a four-year institution, or to find employment after leaving. It becomes a distributing agency between secondary school and various social institutions. b) As it comes to discharge these functions, it tends to effect a reorganization of American education; for students who at least complete the Bachelor's Degree the pattern of education becomes an 8-4-2-2 instead of 8-4-4. In addition, the role of the community college in its democratization of postsecondary education, the open door policy, low cost to students, adult education and community service all combine to make the community college the most effective educational vehicle today in extending education opportunities. More than any

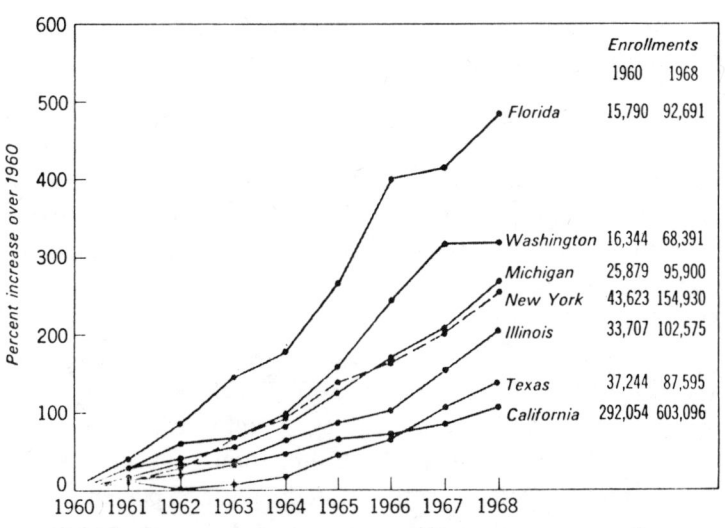

	Enrollments	
	1960	1968
Florida	15,790	92,691
Washington	16,344	68,391
Michigan	25,879	95,900
New York	43,623	154,930
Illinois	33,707	102,575
Texas	37,244	87,595
California	292,054	603,096

SOURCE: American Association of Junior Colleges.

Relative growth of community college enrollments, 1960-1968, for seven pacesetter states

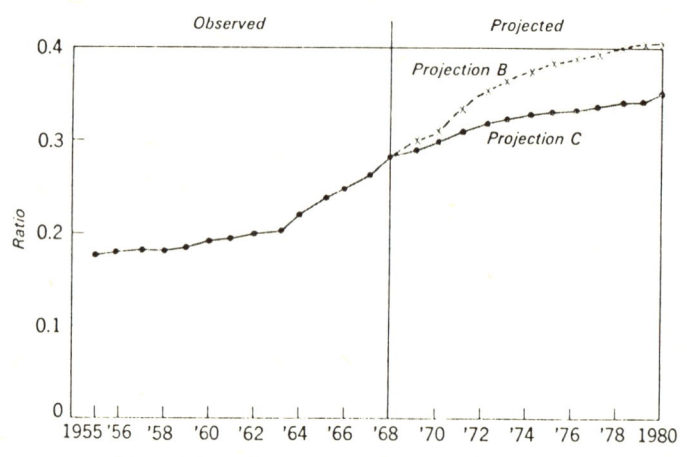

[Graph: Observed and projected ratios of junior college enrollments to total undergraduate enrollments, 1955–1980. Y-axis: Ratio (0 to 0.4). Observed curve rises from ~0.18 in 1955 to ~0.30 in 1968. Projected curves: Projection B rises to ~0.38 by 1980; Projection C rises to ~0.35 by 1980.]

SOURCE: Adapted from the working papers of Gus Haggstrom for the Carnegie Commission on Higher Education. Projected ratios are based on enrollment projections B and C as discussed on page 28.

Observed and projected ratios of junior college enrollments to total undergraduate enrollments

other segment of the educational system, it has the freedom to experiment, to explore new paths of learning, to break with traditional methods of teaching and to become a unique and innovative educational agency.[28]

Stressing "the profound changes in the social structure where in the past the campus has been a kind of youth ghetto," Chancellor Boyer of the State University of New York calls attention to the fact that "more and more college age youth are rejecting the seemingly endless incubation of full-time formal education for a more rewarding pattern of work and study. Over 55 percent of all those enrolled in postsecondary education today are part-time students." He sees this as a breaking up of a rigid life cycle with enormous implications for higher education. Higher education is viewed "not as a prework ritual, but as a resource for everyone from 18 to 85 and beyond." He looks for new approaches to recurring education, developed in partnership with business, industry and labor. "All Americans," he feels "should have periodic opportunities to enrich themselves intellectually and refine their work skills. Higher education has the opportunity to add another freedom to the Four Freedoms—the freedom to learn whatever the age, whatever the stage in life."[29]

During the next ten years business will participate in education to a great extent. Major corporations are already contracted to teach marketable skills to the deprived and reclaim slums. John Kenneth Galbraith has noted that the modern corporation already has the power to shape society. Hazel Henderson commented in the Harvard Business Review that industry's expansion into such areas as housing, education and dropout training is probably the best way to handle our central core city needs if suitable performance standards and general specifications are properly controlled. The growth of a cooperative business and education relationship is seen as being of great portent in the seventies as corporations expand the production activities of the education industry and assume more management and control responsibilities.[30]

Quality of Education

Many in the community college field, like President O'Connell of Berkshire Community College and Dr. Robert R. Gwydir, Jr. of Nassau Community College in Garden City, Long Island, have said the measure of equality is how well their graduates do in good four-year institutions they transfer to as juniors, "and as a matter of fact they do well."[31] President O'Connell found in the community college a particularly fascinating group in the students of lower middle class or working class families whose cultural backgrounds are severely limited. They are the first generation college-going people. Their parents could never even have considered college themselves and may even have felt threatened by the potential change of values and social mobility as their children enter the new world of higher education.[32]

Visiting with Dr. Gwydir I learned that Nassau Community does not have an open door policy "because they cannot accommodate them. Much will depend also upon its success in urban areas." A new campus, however, is presently going up, slated for completion for the Fall of 1978—to accommodate over 10,000 day students. Nassau Community College has moved from almost a total liberal arts program now to a posture of a comprehensive community college in answer to the needs of the community. It now typifies the comprehensive community college as "trying to fit all the needs of the community, and still growing." "Students are more career oriented, more pragmatic, when they go out in the world, they want to be better prepared, with some training. They seriously question the relevance of the liberal arts program." For those who want to teach, Dr. Gwydir stresses "the community college is where it now is at. The emphasis is on teaching, and while research and publication are important and professional, the emphasis in the community college is on teaching. Both students and faculty are actively involved in governance. The Academic Senate with representatives from all departments includes 15 students who have a voice in governance and vote. Students at Nassau Community College do have a real role in governance. All committees have relevance for them.[33]

"I came to Staten Island Community College knowing virtually nothing about the two year college," declared its president William M. Birenbaum. "There was a growing mood in the public policy to offer the junior college as the equal educational opportunity for minority group youth." Staten Island Community College is an open door college—it is committed to let anyone in who has earned any high school diploma. Dr. Birenbaum's philosophy is "everyone can be educated and should be to the full limit of his abilities." At this city university there is no tuition fee; there are 225,000 students on an annual budget of a half-billion dollars, and currently committed to construct new buildings and campuses costing more than a billion and a half. Large numbers of people from social classes never before admitted to the university are getting in. Dr. Birenbaum declares, "They are asking questions about what they have gotten in to. Some lack basic skills in mathematics, languages and the sciences. They are demanding now the opportunities for learning that have for some time been available to other classes in our nation."[34]

Egalitarianism in Higher Education

Medsker and Tillery are in accord with the final report of the Carnegie Commission concerning the issue of better understanding and implementation of the new concept of egalitarianism in Higher Education. To fully implement the egalitarian principle, there is agreement of a change necessary in the concept of education beyond the high school from that of Higher Education as it has been known to that of postsecondary education, which embraces an array of institutions and programs even more diverse than we have had to date. The community college is seen as being in the forefront of these institutions, being among several offering opportunities for non-baccalaureate study.[35]

In 1971, David Bushnell of Project Focus administered statements of institutional goals to samples of faculty, students, and presidents of 92 public and private two-year colleges that constituted a reasonable representative sample of the national population of two year institutions.

Students seem to be rejecting the traditional notion of teaching subject matter for its own sake in favor of a more flexible approach of teaching the attitudes and skills of learning. Community college faculty are usually less discipline-bound and therefore more hospitable to this conception of learning than are university faculty who are committed to advancing knowledge in their academic specialty. The name change from junior to community colleges for most public two-year institutions reflects a commitment to serve the local community and Bushnell reports that faculty, students, and administrators accept that commitment. They not only think their college should serve local needs, but they are convinced that it does stress a community orientation.[36]

Students in the Bushnell survey think that their community college should (and does) provide some form of education for any student regardless of academic ability and that the college should (and does) make financial assistance available to any student who wants to enroll in college. Faculty and presidents show some evidence of backlash to egalitarianism, however. They think that some egalitarian goals are receiving somewhat higher priority than they should; faculty would demote the goal of working with students of any ability level from its present emphasis of 2nd place to a preferred rank of 7th out of 12 goals. Presidents would demote it from 14th to 18th place out of 26 goals.

Perhaps the most significant finding with regard to equality of opportunity is the firm rejection of any kind of quota system on the part of all community college groups, including students. Allocating a percent of enrollment to minority groups or those of low socioeconomic status ranks at or near the bottom on everyone's list as does the goal of attracting a representative number of minority faculty.

Students, faculty, and presidents in community colleges across the nation say that they do not presently assign much priority to egalitarian goals that imply preferential treatment for certain groups, and furthermore, they don't think they should.[37]

Faculty Commitment

Because the community college cannot be equated with college in the traditional sense, many educators call for greater faculty commitment to community college programs. Medsker's suggestion is for the development of new programs in American universities to prepare college faculty for understanding better the role of the community college in higher education. There is the feeling that "faculty must be committed to the democratization of the community college instructional program, if there are to be open door colleges in truth rather than in fiction. The open door equal access philosophy brings into college many students who may need individualized instruction and thus mandates a change in the approach to teaching."[38]

From the point of view of Professor Cohen "traditional faculty members are making a desperate attempt to plant sprigs of ivy so that the barbarians will be dissuaded from entering." He sees the need for educators to join the ranks with other professors in a common effort to solve these problems. "Why," declares Cohen, "should ignorant, culturally deprived youth be branded undesirable because they are academically inept and need education desperately?"[39] Since the main function of the community college instructor is to teach Cohen maintains, "he must be committed to this role and specialize in the instructional process." In fact he is firm in stating that "if teaching remedial or developmental courses are below their dignity then they do not belong in the community college. Cohen makes a crucial point that many community college instructors persist in the practice of norm-referenced testing and curve-based grade marking practices. He states these traditional methods assume from the start that all will not succeed. His position is such practices have no place in any community college that is willing to open its door and be accountable for its learning. Research shows that specifying learning objectives in precise terms and using well-organized, self-paced instructional sequences to reach those objectives can guarantee learning for up to 90 percent of all students.[40]

Accountability

Until recently this belief in a limited or predetermined capacity to learn precluded the idea of accountability for learning. How can anyone with the possible exception of the learner who might be lazy and therefore fail to utilize all of his capacity be held accountable for something determined by heredity? It would certainly be unreasonable to hold educators accountable for something over which they had no control.

Currently this belief in educational determinism is being discarded. Studies have revealed self-fulfilling tendencies in the measurement of student achievement where educators are informed in advance of student "intelligence quotients or learning abilities." Given the evidence of many studies and the re-examination of basic beliefs about learning, there is growing recognition that almost all students can learn if a variety of instructional approaches are available and if sufficient time is allowed each student. Associate Commissioner Leon Lessinger before he left the United States Office of Education in January 1970 reinforced the findings of the Coleman Report of 1966 when he indicated that the disparity of cultural background skills between socioeconomic classes makes equal opportunity a sham. The report further stated those who have already been deprived of opportunities to develop culturally cannot achieve equal educational results even when they are provided identical schooling. "A policy of educational equality must consider inputs (racial balance), comparability of resources, but that true equality can only be judged by outputs (equity of results)." The report advanced the idea that schools should be evaluated and educators be held accountable on the basis of student performance accountability.

Accountability assumes and shifts responsibility. Students have traditionally been held responsible for whatever they may or may not have learned. Accountability shifts the emphasis of that responsibility away from the student. Another associate commissioner, Don Davis, said, "The concept of accountability links student performance with teacher performance. . . . It means . . . that schools and colleges will be judged by how they perform not by what they promise. It means . . . shifting primary learning responsibility from the student to the school."[41]

The community college movement is seen as being much more than a democratically inspired attempt to meet educational demands that have been ignored by other institutions of higher learning. Postsecondary education in the United States today is a vital national need—not a luxury. The community college is in the unique position to answer that need. The role of unskilled workers becomes less important as technological society grows more complex. There is also an insistent national demand for manpower trained in sophisticated skills. The nation today cannot afford to waste human resources. Educational institutions have the responsibility of imparting essential skills to all students. What can be stressed is that "there is a marked difference between allowing a disadvantaged youth to learn and taking responsibility for the direction and extent of that learning." A concomitant among educators is that accountability will also require a change in the attitude of governance and administration, and particularly in the attitude of instructors. According to Cohen, if teachers refuse to spell out ends or accept accountability for achievement, the enterprise will not succeed.[42]

Gleazer, writing in the Educational Record, winter of 1970, feels the question is not whether a student is college material. He addresses himself rather to questions like "can we come up with . . . the professional attitudes . . . necessary to put us into the business of tapping pools of human talent not yet touched?" He feels the clear statement of accountability strikes at the heart of the community college problem. Sharing Cohen's concern, Gleazer feels the promise of the "open door" will never be realized until teachers change their attitudes and accept the professional responsibility of becoming accountable for students. He sees the need for accountability to permeate every level of the institution, and concurs with Cohen in that "the individual instructor is by far the most important element in the success of the community college program."[43]

Examples of Community Colleges with Educational Accountability

Pursuing the philosophy of educational accountability, South Oklahoma City Junior College demands that educators tell their students what they will receive in exchange for their time and tuition dollars. Among the innovations are mastery learning, instead of competitive grading, full accountability for learning instead of none, individually paced instruction of students instead of one-track pacing of student progress, and open admissions.[44]

Under the leadership of its founding president, Thomas M. Hatfield, the trustees of John Tyler Community College in Chester, Virginia, more than a year ago issued a strong policy statement regarding educational accountability. At John Tyler Community College, the president is held responsible for the outcome of the educational program. Brookdale Community College, Lincroft, New Jersey, are committed to total educational accountability. Dr. Erwin Harlacher of Brookdale Community College is professionally committed to using student success as the measure of evaluating the presidential office and other college personnel. Moraine Valley Community College, Palos Hills, Illinois, is another two year college building its educational program on accountability. Dr. Robert Turner, its president is committed to making the "open door" concept a reality for the students his college serves. All college personnel, instructional, administrative, and support staff, develop measurable objectives against which their performance is evaluated.[45]

Kittrell, Mitchell and Mount Olive Junior College all serve as excellent examples of private institutions that have for more than one year been working at accountability. Kittrell's president, sharing an opinion with many other private college leaders including Roueche, Baker and Brownell, feels that a college committed to real educational accountability may soon be able to recruit prospective students on a "money back guarantee." If the student does not succeed, the college would be willing to refund part or all of the student's money. Guaranteed learning is the goal for many private colleges which consider accountability an opportunity for maximizing educational effectiveness. It is not viewed as a threat, but rather as a tool for achieving the college's mission.[45]

What Is the Mission of the Community College?

What is its mission, who is it to serve? This is a serious issue, according to Dr. Gleazer. For the 70s, he sees the community college entering a new period in its evolution. He looks for the movement to broaden beyond academic studies, vocational training and open admissions.[46] A view equally shared by President Harlacher of Brookdale Community College—he sees ahead that through its informal community dimension function it will truly become a community college. Chancellor Samuel B. Gould of the State University of New York emphasized this when he said that "a college in addition to its more readily accepted intellectual dimension should have the dimension of community that offers a place for the general enrichment of all who live nearby."[47]

After visiting thirty-seven community colleges during the Summer and Fall of 1967, Dr. Harlacher found the community college represents a newness in education, a new try at making a local educational institution a real and vital part of the community of people who support it. Both educators see for the future the community college placing a greater emphasis on the "community dimension." It will begin to show that community services are "designed to take the college program out into the community as well as bring the community to the college."

Summarizing the Role of the Community College for the 70s

The community colleges have a crucial role to play in Higher Education for the 70s, 1) as an innovative educational agency, 2) as a vital source of continuing Postsecondary Education and 3) demonstrating leadership in regard to open admissions as recommended by the Carnegie Commission in its final report for 1973. The areas which hold the Commission's special attention are the metropolitan areas where the need is greatest. The Commission also sees the need for a wider spread of community colleges across the nation so that 95 percent of all persons will be within commuting distance of a college.

It is not too difficult to understand and appreciate the concern of many in the middle class who are better equipped to meet existing educational criteria for college admissions and who resent open admissions. In our democratic society, however, we view social mobility through education; every one has a right to seek higher education. The person who has a high school diploma is entitled to and should be given the opportunity to better himself. Actually, the entrance examinations in themselves do not determine whether a student will make it. The socially disadvantaged persons as well as adults returning to school for whatever motivation deserve support for whatever assistance they need to fulfill their academic or vocational goals. This need for greater availability of space and change of attitude on the part of instructors stands out as a challenge. There is also the need to spell out the right and guarantee of a Higher Education, supported by the commitment of both faculty and educators alike in Higher Education. There are many who hold the Right to an Education is one of the most important but undefined of the Bill of Rights. I share that view. Who can deny that both specialized training and Higher Education are vehicles to advancement, and are basic in our technology society? This concern for greater availability of opportunity is equally spelled out by the Crossland Ford Foundation Report of 1971, the Coleman Report of 1966, and the 1972 and 1973 reports of the Carnegie Commission. What educators like Medsker, Tillery, Gleazer, Birenbaum, Cohen are saying is that the open door policy can expose these people to experiences they have never known before. Education can give them options. Every effort should be made to assist them to succeed.

To the degree that instructors utilize the time, effort and commitment to dedicated teaching, I feel accountability is crucial. Another factor is the low expectation value, characteristic of the attitude of many teachers as supported by various studies of student performance from poor backgrounds. This can be prejudicial, capable of influencing teacher performance and student capability and output. Evelyn B. Whitaker, once classified "academically disadvantaged," is presently an assistant Dean at New York City Community College in Brooklyn, and director of counseling for the 17,000 student campus. Her own accomplishments were partly the result of the guidance of teachers who "had faith in her ability to overcome a poor academic background."

Through its community service function, the community college is seen as breaking the lockstep of tradition, that is, college is semester length, courses, credits, culturally and educationally elite. It is also dedicated to the proposition, important as are the formalized curricula offered in the classroom, information provided on a continuous basis through the community for all of the rest of the people is of equal importance.

How effectively community colleges handle some of the issues in the final analysis is still a matter of individual community college goal priorities. Viewing, however, its non-traditional orientation, flexibility of programs and broad comprehensiveness of curricula, the community college today is in a unique position in Higher Education. It has the opportunity to provide leadership and play a significant role in serving all the educational needs of the community. Will it meet the challenge?

BIBLIOGRAPHY

Birenbaum, Dr. William M. *Something for Everybody is Not Enough*. New York: Random House, 1971.

—— "From Class to Mass—Sociology and the Sciences of Education," Sixth Congress of the International Association of Sciences and Education, Sorbonne, Paris, September 3-7, 1973, 5.

Boyer, Ernest L., "Higher Education for All, Through Old Age," *The New York Times*, April 8, 1974, 35.

Cohen, Arthur M. Dateline 79: *Heretical Concepts for the Community College*. Beverly Hills, California: The Glencoe Press, 1969.

Cross, K. Patricia, "What Do You Know About the Goals of the Community College," *Community College Journal*, April 1974, 35.

Crossland, Fred E. Ford Foundation Report. New York: Schocken Books, 1971.

Facing Facts About the Two Year College. Prudential Life Insurance Company of America, 1973.

Fields, Ralph R. *The Community College Movement*. New York: McGraw Hill Book Company, 1962.

Gleazer, Edmund J. Jr. *This is the Community College*. Boston: Houghton, Mifflin Company, 1968.

—— "After the Boom . . . What Now for the Community College," *Community and Junior College Journal*, December-January, 1973.

Gwyder, Dr. Robert R. Nassau Community College. Interview February 19, 1974.

Harlacher, Ervin L. *The Community Dimension on the Community College*. Englewood Cliffs, New Jersey: Prentice-Hall, Inc., 1969.

Hofstader, Richard and Hardy, C. De Witt. *The Development and Scope of Higher Education in the United States*. New York: Columbia University Press, 1952.

Jacqueney, Mona G. *Radicalism on Campus: 1969-1971*. New York: Philosophical Library, 1972.

Medsker, Leland and Tillery, Dale. *Breaking the Access Barrier: A Profile of Two Year Colleges*. New York: McGraw Hill Book Company, 1971.

Monroe, Charles R. *Profile of the Community College*. San Francisco: Jossey-Bass, Inc., 1972.

O'Connell, Thomas E. *Community College: A President's View*. Urbana, Illinois: University of Illinois Press, 1968.

Priorities for Action. Final Report of the Carnegie Commission on Higher Education, 1973.

Roeuche, John E., Baker, George A. III and Brownell, Richard L. *Accountability and the Community College: Directions for the 70s*. American Association of Community and Junior Colleges, Washington, D.C., 1972.

Shane, Harold G. and Shane, June Grant. "Forecasts for the 70s," *Technology in Education: Challenge and Change*. Worthington, Ohio: Charles A. Jones Publishing Company, 1972.

The Campus and the City. The Carnegie Commission Report on Higher Education, 1972.

Towards A Learning Society: Alternate Channels to Life, Work and Service. Carnegie Commission Report, October, 1973.

FOOTNOTES

[1]Richard Hofstader and C. De Witt Hardy, *The Development and Scope of Higher Education in the United States*, New York: Columbia University Press, 1952, 141-142.

[2]Arthur M. Cohen, *Dateline '79: Heretical Concepts for the Community College*, The Glencoe Press: Beverly Hills, California, 1969, Preface XVI.

[3]Leland L. Medsker and Dale Tillery, *Breaking the Access Barriers: A Profile of Two Year Colleges*, New York: McGraw Hill Book Co., 1971, 69.

[4]*Priorities for Action*, Final Report of the Carnegie Commission on Higher Education, 1973, 29.

[5]Edmund J. Gleazer, Jr., *This is the Community College*, Boston: Houghton, Mifflin Co., 1968, 4.

[6]Medsker and Tillery, 10.

[7]*Ibid.*, 57.

[8]*Facing Facts About the Two Year College*, Prudential Life Insurance Company of America, 1973, 30.

[9]Mona G. Jacqueney, *Radicalism on Campus: 1969-1971*, New York: Philosophical Library, 1972, 75.

[10]*Facing Facts About the Two Year College*, 17.

[11]Medsker and Tillery, 11.

[12]*Ibid.*, 64-65.

[13]*Ibid.*, 105.

[14]Ralph R. Fields, *The Community College Movement*, New York: McGraw Hill Book Company, 1962, 55, 62.

[15]Thomas E. O'Connell, *Community College: A President's View*, Urbana, Illinois: University of Illinois Press, 1968, 2, 5.

[16]Charles R. Monroe, *Profile of the Community College*, San Francisco: Jossey-Bass, Inc., 1972, 14.

[17]Gleazer, 14.

[18]Medsker and Tillery, 19.

[19]*Ibid.*, 19-20.

[20]Fred E. Crossland, *Ford Foundation Report*, New York: Schocken Books, 1971, lx, 112.

[21] *Priorities for Action*, 35, 76.
[22] Medsker and Tillery, 49.
[23] Monroe, 80, 81.
[24] The Carnegie Commission Report on Higher Education, December 1972, *The Campus and the City*, 38, 46.
[25] *Priorities for Action*, 44, 46-47. *Towards a Learning Society, Alternate Channels to Life, Work and Service*, Carnegie Commission Report October, 1973, 5.
[26] *Priorities for Action*, 87, 132-134.
[27] Medsker and Tillery, 25-27.
[28] *Ibid.*, 136-137.
[29] Ernest L. Boyer, Chancellor of the State University of New York, "Higher Education for All, Through Old Age," *The New York Times*, April 8, 1974, 35.
[30] Harold G. Shane & June Grant Shane, "Forecast for the 70s," *Technology in Education: Challenge & Change*, Worthington, Ohio: Charles A. Jones Publishing Co., 1972, 250.
[31] President O'Connell, 60. Dr. Robert R. Gwydir, Jr., Nassau Community College, interview February 19, 1974.
[32] President O'Connell, 60.
[33] Dr. Robert R. Gwydir, interview 2/19/74.
[34] William M. Birenbaum, *Something for Everybody is Not Enough*, New York: Random House, 1971, 282, 286. Also "From Class to Mass—Sociology and The Science of Education," Dr. William M. Birenbaum, Sixth Congress of the International Association of Sciences and Education, Sorbonne, Paris, Sept. 3-7, 1973, 5.
[35] Medsker and Tillery, 49.
[36] K. Patricia Cross, "What Do You Know About the Goals of Community College, *Community and Junior College Journal*, April 1974, 35.
[37] *Ibid.*
[38] Medsker and Tillery, 147, 158.
[39] Cohen, XVIII.
[40] Cohen, 21, 45, 86, 201.
[41] John E. Roueche, George A. Baker III and Richard L. Brownell, *Accountability and the Community College: Directions for the 70s*, American Association of Community and Junior College, Washington,

D.C., 1972, 6-7. See also Report of the Carnegie Commission of Higher Education, October 1973, 23.
[42]Cohen, 8, 21, 45, 201. Also Roueche, Baker and Brownell, 12.
[43]*Ibid*.
[44]Reid Holland, "Behavioral Objectives and Community College History," *Community and Junior College Journal*, April 1974, 13.
[45]Roueche, Baker and Brownell, 39.
[46]Edmund J. Gleazer, Jr. "After the Boom . . . What Now for the Community College," reprinted from December-January *Community and Junior College Journal*, 1973.
[47]Ervin L. Harlacher, *The Community Dimension of the Community College*, Englewood Cliffs, N.J.: Prentice-Hall Inc., 1969, 3, 69.